SQUADRONS!

No. 16

THE NORTH AMERICAN
MITCHELL
- THE DUTCH, FRENCH AND POLES -

PHIL H. LISTEMANN

ISBN: 978-2918590-98-9

www.RAF-IN-COMBAT.com

Colour profiles: Gaetan Marie/Bravo Bravo Aviation

GLOSSARY OF TERMS

PERSONEL :

(AUS)/RAF: Australian serving in the RAF
(BEL)/RAF: Belgian serving in the RAF
(CAN)/RAF: Canadian serving in the RAF
(CZ)/RAF: Czechoslovak serving in the RAF
(NFL)/RAF: Newfoundlander serving in the RAF
(NL)/RAF: Dutch serving in the RAF
(NZ)/RAF: New Zealander serving in the RAF
(POL)/RAF: Pole serving in the RAF
(RHO)/RAF: Rhodesian serving in the RAF
(SA)/RAF: South African serving in the RAF
(US)/RAF - RCAF : American serving in the RAF or RCAF

RANKS

G/C : Group Captain
W/C : Wing Commander
S/L : Squadron Leader
F/L : Flight Lieutenant
F/O : Flying Officer
P/O : Pilot Officer
W/O : Warrant Officer
F/Sgt : Flight Sergeant
Sgt : Sergeant
Cpl : Corporal
LAC : Leading Aircraftman

OTHER

ATA: Air Transport Auxiliary
CO : Commander
DFC : Distinguished Flying Cross
DFM : Distinguished Flying Medal
DSO : Distinguished Service Order
Eva. : Evaded
ORB : Operational Record Book
OTU : Operational Training Unit
PoW : Prisoner of War
PAF: Polish Air Force
RAF : Royal Air Force
RAAF : Royal Australian Air Force
RCAF : Royal Canadian Air Force
RNZAF : Royal New Zealand Air Force
SAAF : South African Air Force
s/d: Shot down
Sqn : Squadron
† : Killed

THE NORTH AMERICAN MITCHELL

The Mitchell was one of the major medium bombers of the Second World War. It was ordered off the drawing board in September 1939, being a development of North American's 1938 NA-40 design. There was no XB-25 prototype and the first of 24 B-25s, powered by two 1,700hp Cyclone engines, made its maiden flight on 19 August 1940. The B-25As that followed were similar, apart from some internal improvements, and forty of this version had been built and were in service, at the time of the attack on Pearl Harbor. Production of 119 B-25Bs was underway but, although this version became famous for its participation in the Doolittle Tokyo raid, it was not really combat ready despite changes made to the armament. The RAF received 23 as the Mitchell Mk. I (**FK161-FK183**). This mark was soon followed by the B-25C (built at Inglewood, California) and D (built at Kansas City, Kansas) which were largely similar to the B apart from the engines and further internal changes. Those two versions were widely used until the end of the war and eventually 1,619 B-25Cs and 2,290 B-25Ds were produced. The RAF used the same denomination for both variants, Mitchell Mk. II, of which 476 were allocated RAF serials:
FL164-FL218 (55), **FL671-FL709** (39), **FR362-FR384** (23), **FR393-FR397** (5), **FV900-FW280** (281), **HD302-HD345** (44), **KL133-KL161** (29). Also, two more Mitchells, en route to the NEI and isolated in India, were taken over by the RAF in 1942 and received the serials **MA956** and **MA957**, but retained their identities as B-25Cs.

Unlike its competitor, the Martin B-26 Marauder, the Mitchell was widely exported and deliveries were also made to the air forces of the Soviet Union, the Netherlands, Brazil, Canada and Australia. Even the US Marine Corps introduced its own version, the PBJ, which saw action in the Pacific. The conventional bomber versions were followed by the unconventional, but pioneering, B-25G, of which 405 were produced. This mark was famously equipped with a 75mm cannon carried in a 'solid' nose. The RAF received two for evaluation (**FR208** and **FR209**), but no RAF mark was assigned. The 1,000 B-25Hs that followed were an improved version of the B-25G and utilised a lighter weight 75mm cannon and was also equipped with fourteen 0.50in machine-guns and provision for a torpedo or 3,200 lb of bombs. This made this variant one of the most heavily armed aircraft in the world. However, the use of the 75mm cannon was slowly phased out during the war. This version led to the last wartime version, the B-25J, which was to become the most numerous variant. In production from late 1943 to the end of the war, a total of 4,318 were built. Production ended after VJ-Day. This model reverted to the bombing role, but apart from its transparent nose, and modified armament, it was similar to the B-25H. It could also be fitted with a solid gun nose and excelled in the ground attack strafer role. It entered in RAF as the Mitchell Mk. III and the following serials were allocated:
HD346-HD401 (56), **KJ561-KJ800** (240), **KP308-KP328** (21), for a total of 371.
The B-25 was the most widely used Allied medium bomber during W.W.II and saw action on all fronts. In RAF markings, Mitchells flew more than 17,000 operational sorties, of which 2,700 were flown by the Mitchell Mk. III. Despite its improvements, the Mk. III was less popular with the crews in general as they found it heavier and less responsive than the Mk. II.

THE DUTCH CONTRACT
The RAF bought the Mitchell to replace the Douglas Boston then in service, but approaching obsolescence. The introduction written above will lead to a specific publication that will be totally dedicated to the Mitchell's RAF career (Nos 98, 180 and 226 Squadrons). Interestingly, a batch of serials was not connected to the RAF, but to the Dutch - **FR141-FR152** (12) and **FR156-FR207** (52). This batch was actually the property of the Dutch government in exile and not lend-lease aircraft supplied to the British.

The B-25C/Ds were the first true combat ready variants of the Mitchell. Here FL191 is seen, while being tested by the A&AEE, marked with an unusual 'P' which was applied to all aircraft for which there were no 'Pilot's notes', so included many aircraft other than actual true prototypes. The aircraft was wrecked in an accident on 1 October 1942. The Mitchell Mk. II entered operational service in January 1943.

Mitchell HD361 was one of the three Mk.IIIs taken on RAF charge and was used by the A&AEE to assess the new variant. The Mk.III was the RAF version of the B-25J. This model would see wide usage after the war and was supplied to many air forces, mainly in Latin America. Note the of absence of gun pods, two 0.50in on each side, normally located below the cockpit. The RAF removed this installation as it was found to be of no use in Europe. The Mk. III was first used in operations in November 1944.

The Dutch were the first export customer of the Mitchell. On 30 June 1941, the Netherlands Purchasing Commission (NPC) ordered 162 B-25Cs to be used in the Netherlands East Indies (NEI). This purchase was eventually approved by an American government, that was at first reluctant, with the aim to reinforce potential allies in the face of the increasing threat of an expansion of the Empire of Japan. The aircraft were paid for in cash and the batch received the North American denomination of NA-90. Deliveries were scheduled to start in November 1942, and had to be completed in February 1943, but the delivery of B-25s on order for the USAAC had to take precedence. However, when war reached Southeast Asia in December 1941, the NPC requested an accelerated delivery plan that was duly accepted. When the NEI fell in March 1942, the first Mitchells were already on their way to the region. These aircraft were eventually diverted to Australia and their presence would lead to the formation of No. 18 (NEI) Squadron RAAF later in the year. More Dutch Mitchells arrived in Australia and it soon became clear that there would not be enough Dutch flying personnel to make use of all of the 162 Mitchells ordered. Some aircraft were transferred to the RAAF to convert No. 2 Squadron RAAF onto type (see Allied Wings No. 9), but, even with that, there were still too many Mitchells. The US government offered to divert a part of the order to the UK where other Dutch aircrew were fighting with the RAF. There was only one operational squadron actually, No. 320 (Dutch) Squadron, which had been formed in June 1940 from former Royal Netherlands Naval Air Service (RNNAS) personnel evacuated to Britain. The squadron was placed under Coastal Command authority and carried out patrols with ex-Dutch Fokker T.VIIIs before receiving Avro Ansons. In 1943, the squadron was re-equipped with Lockheed Hudsons. The Dutch government in exile accepted the offer and, in accordance with the RAF, the squadron was transferred from Coastal Command to Bomber Command with the aim of integrating the newcomer into the future 2 TAF (which is where it would become operational during the summer of 1943). The squadron was unique in being the only 2 TAF unit to be fully-manned by naval personnel. However, the reserve of personnel became an issue in 1944, as losses for a bomber squadron are, of course, much higher than for a general reconnaissance squadron. From the end of the summer of 1944, the gaps were filled with Belgian personnel or other RAF or Dominion aircrew.

Of the 64 Mitchells diverted to the UK for the Dutch, one was actually retained by the US (FR187), and two were lost during the ferry flight (FR148 and FR203), leaving only 61 aircraft to be allocated to 320 Squadron. It was a mixed bag of B-25Cs and Ds - B-25C-10 (24), B-25C-15 (4), B-25C-20 (4), B-25C-25 (4), B-25D-20 (16) and B-25D-25 (12). The range of variants, and sub-variants, only differed in minor details and equipment fit-out. The losses sustained in the first year of operations meant that almost all of the Dutch Mitchells would see operational service with the squadron by the end of war. Some aircraft achieved a high number of sorties and flying hours. Such intensive use, and with the aim of preserving some airframes for post-war usage some RAF Mitchells were included in the squadron's inventory from the end of summer 1944. Some Mk. IIs were the first to arrive, but were followed by Mk. IIIs. As the squadron had become a mixed Dutch, non-Dutch squadron by that time, it was logical to see RAF Mitchells allocated to the squadron. There was no stress on the RAF's inventory as plenty of Mitchells were stored at various MUs. However, it must be added that of the 61 Mitchells made available for the squadron, only 25 would be transferred to the Netherlands in July 1947.

March 1943
August 1945

Number of sorties: *ca.* **3,920**

First operational sortie:
12.06.43
Last operational sortie:
02.05.45

Number of claims: *nil*

Total aircraft written-off: 34

Aircraft lost on operations: 31
Aircraft lost in accidents: 3

Squadron code letters:
NO

COMMANDING OFFICERS

Cdr Karel J.A. Meester	RNNAS	...	20.09.43
Cdr Eduard Bakker (†)	RNNAS	20.09.43	25.10.43
LtCdr Jack F. Breedveld (Temp.)	RNNAS	26.10.43	21.12.43
Cdr Hugo V.B. Burgerhout	RNNAS	21.12.43	29.06.44
LtCdr Johan N. Mulder (Temp.)	RNNAS	29.06.44	07.09.44
Cdr Hugo V.B. Burgerhout	RNNAS	07.09.44	28.12.44
Cdr Arent W. Witholt	RNNAS	28.12.44	...

SQUADRON USAGE

The first of three Dutch squadrons to be raised in England was No. 320 Squadron. Manned by former Royal Netherlands Naval Air Service personnel evacuated to Britain, it was logically used for coastal defence duties (later reinforced with former Dutch Air Force personnel - WLM). The CO was Commander (Wing Commander) K.J.A. Meester. The big move took place on 15 March when the squadron moved from RAF Bircham Newton to RAF Methwold. The first two Mitchells, FR143 and FR149, arrived two days later and were followed by FR147 on the 19th and FR144 on the 20th. Over the next few days, a complement of personnel arrived, 24 Wireless Operators, while other airmen were sent to complete a course of flight mechanics or gunnery. The first two training flights were flown on the 23rd. In April, training intensified with more than 450 training sorties performed while other Mitchells were taken on charge (FR142, FR168, FR208, FL168, FL202, FL679 and FL686). In May and June, FR148, FR169, FR170, FR173 and FR174 arrived to make up the initial establishment of sixteen Mitchells. The number of training flights could now increase, with more than 600 flown in May and over 550 in June. The squadron had an unexpected operational debut on 12 June when six aircraft were called upon for an Air Sea Rescue mission. Twelve more were shipped out for the same task on the 25th. By June, the squadron became part of an operational structure that would evolve into No. 139 Wing by D-Day. In July 1943, training continued with over 600 flights, including further ASR missions on the 26th, 28th and 30th. Sadly, FR144 did not return from one of these flights. The crew, captained by LtCdr W.J. Ritte, sighted a raft and

Commander Karel Meerster was the CO when 320 Sqn was transferred to 2 TAF for conversion to the Mitchell. He had taken over the squadron in June 1942 and, at 41, was one of the oldest Coastal Command COs at the time. He was a long-serving Dutch naval officer who had been stationed in the NEI in December 1941.

5

Mitchells of 320 Sqn being prepared at Lasham for another Ramrod during the summer of 1943. In the foreground is FR157/X with FR166/R behind. FR157 would survive the war while FR166 was lost the following 25 October. *(via Chris Thomas)*

turned around to investigate. The pilot made a sharp turn towards the raft and obviously pulled the Mitchell out too late with the result being that the port wing touched the water and the aircraft cartwheeled in. No sign of any survivors was observed and the only trace of the Mitchell and its crew was a half-inflated dinghy. This was the first loss sustained by the Dutch while flying the Mitchell. Up to mid-August, another 200 flights were flown before the squadron was ready to be put into action. ASR sorties were also flown on the 3rd and 16th. On 17 August, the first operation was carried out when six Mitchells participated in the bombing of marshalling yards at Calais in France (this kind of op was called a *Ramrod*: short range bomber attacks to destroy ground targets). All of the aircraft, led by Lt P. van Waart, returned safely to base after two hours and the mission was rather uneventful. The CO led the next mission when twelve Mitchells bombed the Luftwaffe aerodrome at Poix. Here, too, no air opposition was encountered nor flak experienced and the squadron was back at base after two and a half hours. The next day, the squadron, with twelve more Mitchells, was airborne and head-

Left, W/C Lewis Lynn was posted to 320 Sqn to supervise its transition to operations. Due to the lack of combat experience among the Dutch aircrew, he participated in numerous ops with the squadron until mid-January 1944. He had previously served with 107 Sqn on Bostons in 1942 where he received the DFC. He was awarded the DSO in February 1944 and added a Bar to it in July 1944 as WingCo Flying of 139 Wing. Right, Commander Eduard Bakker seen shortly after he took over the squadron in September 1943. He was killed one month later. Bakker was among the Dutch naval personnel to flee to the UK in May 1940 and soon formed the squadron using Fokker T. VIIIs. He was to spend all of his operational career in the RAF with 320.

Another scene of 320 Squadron's Mitchells lined up at Larsham in December 1943. Mitchell NO-D was FR149 and was lost on 12 June 1944 over Normandy after completing 52 ops. It had been christened 'Hollandsche Nieuwe' (New Holland). Just next to it, FR205/NO-O was lost in action the following day, the 13th. The Dutch Mitchells carried the Dutch triangle on both sides.

(via Chris Thomas)

ing for the Dornier Aircraft works at Flushing (Netherlands). This time, heavy and accurate flak was encountered and FR147/C was soon hit. One shell pierced the left engine which stopped almost immediately. The Mitchell broke formation losing speed and height as the captain, 2nd Lt H. Niemhuis, turned towards the sea with the aim of getting as far from the Dutch coast as possible. The Mitchell was actually so badly damaged that a return flight home was impossible, and Niemhuis warned the crew, and the controller, that he had no choice but to ditch the aircraft into the sea. The captain successfully ditched the aircraft and all of the crew had time to escape into the dinghy. The Mitchell sunk after floating for eight minutes. The crew was immediately rescued by a Walrus. The rest of the squadron returned safely to base after another two and a half hour op. For the rest of the month the squadron was released from operations and only flew some ASR sorties on the 23rd and 25th. At the end of the month, the unit was relocated to Lasham near Alton. This would be its base for the next six months.

The squadron was occupied with settling in during the first week of September, but operational flying resumed on the 9th with the bombing of a gun outpost at Boulogne by twelve Mitchells, Cdr Meester leading. The squadron also flew more a total of fifty sorties spread across the 11th, 15th, 18th, 22nd and 24th. In the meantime, on 20 September, a new CO arrived, Commander Bakker. Commander Meester left for the Royal Netherlands Navy HQ in London. However, for some time, Commander Bakker would serve under Wing Commander Lewis A. Lynn, a South African from Transvaal and recipient of the DFC earned while flying Bostons with No. 107 Squadron in 1942. Bakker crewed up and flew with Lynn during this the time to gain experience in this particular role. In the beginning of October, the squadron participated in two *Ramrod* missions (3rd – Le Grand-Quevilly power station near Rouen, and 9th – Guivapas airfield near Brest), both being uneventful. Then, bad weather prevented any operational flying over the continent for the next two weeks. Operations resumed on the 22nd with an abortive op that had to be abandoned due to 10/10 cloud at 7,000 feet. Two days later, an attack was made against Cherbourg docks and the next day another *Ramrod* against the German airfield of Poulmic, near Brest, was flown in conjunction with No. 98 Squadron. The Mitchells experienced heavy and accurate flak over the target which hit the aircraft flown by the Dutch CO of the squadron, Commander Bakker, who was leading the second box (the first was led by W/C Lynn). The Mitchell, FR178/W was seen to burst into flames and break up, leaving no chance of survival for the crew. The explosion damaged a nearby Mitchell, FR162/P, rendering the instruments and hydraulics unserviceable, hitting the right engine and injuring two crew. The Plexiglas in the cockpit was also completely splintered and the pilot was hit in the left arm, but he was able to hold the aircraft straight and level long enough to allow the bomb-aimer to release the bombs. The crippled aircraft then lost height and headed for the English coast where, after a supreme effort, a successful crash landing was made at Perranporth. The Mitchell was later condemned and struck off charge. Another Mitchell (FR166/R) did not return, similarly hit, and the crew was posted missing. It later transpired that the cap-

A Dutch Navy crew posing in front of FR141/NO-B, named 'Ouwe Jongens' ('Old Boys'), on 5 March 1944. The squadron was now based at Duxford. This Mitchell was lost two weeks later. From left to right, PO Willem Bijlsma, Lt Jan Grader, WO J.G. Wallis de Vries, and CPO Frans Meijer. All survived the war.
(via Chris Thomas)

tain, Sgt C.J. Banks, was killed and the three other crewmen were taken prisoner. The rest of the formation returned to base after three hours to land at 15.37. The Dutch were particularly unlucky in this op as 98 Squadron returned without having lost a single aircraft. No operational flying was carried out during the next two days, but the Dutch returned to operations to bomb shipping at Cherbourg. Only six Mitchells, led by the CO, joined twelve from 98 Squadron. Flak sealed the fate of FR174/K which was last seen going down over the target. There were no survivors. Two more Mitchells were also severely hit, FR151/C and FR173/J, but both would later return to service. The last week of October had been disastrous for the Dutch. After these losses, the squadron dispatched small numbers of aircraft during the early days of November. Six Mitchells were part of larger formations on the 5th and 8th. The op on the 10th was aborted, and the following day six more Mitchells bombed the village of Auderghem, from 12,000 feet, over which only inaccurate flak was encountered. The squadron was then stood down for the next ten days, mostly because the weather over the Continent prevented effective bombing. Six more Mitchells were then sent to Auderghem again on the 23rd and twelve more returned in the morning two days later. This time, flak damaged FR181/K (Sgt J.H. Maas and crew) and the aircraft returned to base with holes in the right engine nacelle, right rudder and astrodome. Fortunately, none of the crew was injured. Auderghem was visited once more in the afternoon, but the op was

Above, some aircrew, posing for the press in October 1943, faking the walk to the aircraft. Most of the men are smiling or appear in high spirits without any sign of the usual pre-op stress. The Mitchell behind is possibly a new arrival as its individual letter is yet to be painted on and there is no nose gun.
(via André Bar)
Below, not a staged scene, but Mitchell FR165/NO-S being loaded in March 1944 while the crew prepare the aircraft for the next op. FR165 would survive until 9 February 1945 when it was shot down *(via Chris Thomas)*

Mitchell FR191/Y loaded of bombs is taxiing for another raid over German occupied Europe in March/April 1944. This aircraft would be lost on 12 June 1944 in ditching in the Channel. The crew survived.

uneventful. On the 26th, led by W/C Lynn, twelve Mitchells were airborne (one crew flying a borrowed Mitchell from No. 305 Squadron), but the formation was recalled as the escort was unable to make the rendezvous. Another try was made in the afternoon, to attack construction works at Martinvast, with Nos. 98 and 180 Squadrons. This had been one of the first V-weapon launching sites to be spotted and the bomber crews found their target to be strongly defended by extremely accurate flak which shot down FR146/O, with the loss of two crew killed, one becoming a PoW and the fourth evading capture. The squadron could consider itself lucky this time as 180 Squadron lost three Mitchells with none of the twelve crewmen surviving. The last *Ramrod* mission of November took place on the 29th, but it had to be abandoned because of the weather over the target (10/10 cloud with a base at 2,500 feet).

At the end of November, Bakker's successor, Cdr H.V.B. Burgerhaut, was finally posted in. In December, the squadron participated in eight operations, totalling 109 sorties, with all being uneventful. In January, the operational activity increased slightly, with 137 sorties recorded over twelve ops, and then increased again to 170 sorties in fourteen missions in February. Except for some minor flak damage to several aircraft, there was nothing else to report for February other than the move to Dunsford (more or less half-way between Reading and Portsmouth). March began to look like the previous three months, but it seems that the squadron's luck ran out. All started well and the first six raids were completed without incident. On the 18th, however, with 98 Squadron, 320 was dispatched to hit a strongly defended 'Noball' site (V-1) at Gorenflos. The flak was accurate and eight of the squadron's twelve Mitchells were damaged to varying degrees after leaving the target area. The damage sustained by FR177/M was heavy enough to oblige the pilot, 2nd Lt H.T. Voorspuij, to ditch the aircraft into the Channel. The pilot of FR180/H, Sgt J.H. Ot, did the same. Fortunately, both crews survived and were picked up by the ASR services. Two days later, the squadron attacked another 'Noball' target, again in the company of 98 Squadron, and one Mitchell was shot down by flak near Flixecourt. The Mitchell, FR141/B, was seen at 9,000 feet to pull up above the formation after a burst of flak and then dive vertically to explode on the ground near the village of Bourdon. There were no survivors. A Mitchell of 98 Squadron was also lost. The next four operations, which were performed before the end of the month (23rd twice, 26th and 28th), were conducted without any loss. With D-Day approaching, the number of taskings increased for 2 TAF. In April, the squadron's crews participated in 24 *Ramrods*, mostly as a single box of six Mitchells. The most activity came in the last three weeks of the month as the weather prevented any operations over the Continent during the first week of April. No operational losses were reported but, on the 25th, while a joined exercise with night fighters, FR142 was mistakenly shot down by a Mosquito. The Mitchell was badly damaged and the navigator, 2nd Lt Wijtman, bailed out and landed safely. The rest of the crew continued their flight to base, and the pilot, LtCdr Mulder, crash-landed the Mitchell. No injuries to the crew were reported, but the Mitchell was only good for scrap. In May, the squadron flew more than 200 sorties for the first time since the transfer to 2 TAF and this was achieved in 21 operations. There was some cost though. Mitchell, FR184/U, was lost on 4 May. That day, the squadron participated in an attack on Bois de Coquerelles. Hit by flak over the target, FR184 was seen to ditch in the Channel. All of the crew escaped the sinking aircraft and were later picked up by a Walrus.

The Mitchell that was coded 'NO-Z' during the D-Day period was FR185. It is seen here painted in early D-Day markings. This Mitchell was lost on 26 July 1944. However, by D-Day, FR185 had been in service with 320 since November 1943 and had accumulated around fifty ops by that time. Also, the 'Z' has been painted over an earlier letter (note the patch of paint) so this may not be FR185 pictured. *(via Chris Thomas)*

B.58/Melsbroek, 10 November 1944: 320 Squadron' Mitchells lined-up waiting to be serviced. In the forefront a Mitchell II with 58 bomb markings painted on the nose. Even if the individual letter is not visible, at that specific date, only FV970/NO-K is matching with the number of bomb markings. Note the full fuselage stripes which were restored at the end of October 1944 on 2 TAF twin-engine types.

Commander Hugo Burgenhout joined 320 in December 1943, but, after a period of rest between June and September 1944, returned to the squadron to take command until December. A former Do24 unit commander in the NEI, he fought the Japanese until Java fell in March 1942. He managed to avoid capture and reached Australia. He was awarded the DSO in August 1944.

The first days of June were quiet, mainly because of the bad weather prevailing over the Continent, and only two operational night intruder sorties were carried out on the 2nd which also saw the introduction of the Gee-H system, a radio navigation system developed to aid RAF Bomber Command. Twelve more conventional sorties on the night of 5/6 June were then carried out. The squadron participated in D-Day with seventeen sorties, all at night, to attack a bridge near Domfront. The next night, just after midnight, the squadron was engaged to attack railway emplacements at Vire, Montsecret and Flers. Two Mitchells collided over Sussex, FR150/W and FR182/R, and both aircraft crashed, killing both crews in the process. It was, however, the beginning of a dramatic series of events as a third, FR178/T, was posted missing in the morning with all four men on board killed as well. The squadron returned to daylight operations on the 10th to attack a tank concentration at Le Caine, but was then back on night intruder work the following night. On the 12th, late in the afternoon, the squadron was dispatched over the Grimbosq woods and the two villages nearby (Grimbosq and St-Laurent-de-Condel). Mitchell FR149/N was hit by flak near the target. Three of the crew became PoWs while the fourth evaded capture initially but was later captured (van der Heijden). Another Mitchell, FR191/A, was also hit at the same time, but the pilot, LtCdr G. van de Wolf, was able to make a reverse his course and reach the Channel where he ditched. The crew was picked up by a destroyer. The next night, ten Mitchells were dispatched for night intruder ops, to drop flares over different points of enemy held territory, from which FR205/O did not come back. The four crewmembers were posted missing and later declared killed. This first week of operations after D-Day would prove to be costly for the squadron with the loss of six Mitchells. This would, sadly, become the heaviest loss rate sustained by an RAF Mitchell squadron in a week during the war. The following week was loss free, however, even though the squadron was engaged every day with about 150 sorties carried out. By the end of the month, the crews returned exclusively to day operations. Regarded as less dangerous, they were not without danger, and FR151/C was shot down by flak with the loss of its crew. Mitchell FR204/S was also lost on the 24th with no survivors. With such losses (almost half of the operational force) in three weeks and time needed to bolster its complement, the squadron's operational activity was reduced until the end of the month with only six sorties flown. In all, the crews flew over 275 sorties in June with 250 of them being effective.

The squadron was able to fully return to operations from 3 July onwards. That day, fourteen aircraft attacked fuel storage facilities near Argentan. Three Mitchells returned early after losing the formation. An almost daily pressure was maintained during July and August with a series of *Ramrods* flown, but with some night sorties using Gee-H added to the mix. During this period of time, the squadron would lament the loss of FR185/Z, posted missing during the second op of the day on the 26th, and FR158/W during the night of 28/29 July. The latter had been sent alone to attack a gun position south of Caen and never came back. On the 9th of August, it was the turn of FR143/S to be badly damaged by flak while attacking an ammunition depot in the Lyons Forest. It was ditched into the Channel. The crew was rescued, but the navigator was badly wounded in one leg. During the same raid, five other Mitchells were hit and one crewman, in FR186/B, LSM E.E.G. de Preter, was badly wounded. Sadly, he died soon after surgery the following 15 August. On the night of 18/19 August, one of the seven Mitchells detailed for flare dropping over Falaise failed to return (FW258/G) and the crew posted as missing. The month ended with the wreck of FR190 which, due to the wet surface, overran the airfield at Long Newton during a training

'Matrozen' of 320 Squadron pushing a bomb trailer full of 1,000-lb bombs in the autumn 1944.
(*André Bar*)

With engines roaring, the Dutch Mitchells are ready to take-off from B58/Melsbroek. Note the Mitchell on the right with a new paint (but the engine cowling remains in US Olivre Drab), the same aircraft as shown on page 17. It is HD346/NO-V, a Mitchell III. (André Bar)

Winter 1944-1945 was very cold and snowy. Here, ground crews are working at clearing snow from FR199/NO-M. This Mitchell first served as NO-N between June and October 1944 before it suffered an accident on 29 October. Repaired, it returned to the squadron in December as NO-M and would be one of the Mitchells that carried out the last sortie of the war on 2 May 1945. (André Bar)

flight. The fuselage broke aft of the cockpit, both undercarriage legs were wrecked and the tail unit was damaged. While the crew luckily escaped injury, the Mitchell was only good for components. It was also at this time that the first Belgian and British aircrew began to arrive to compensate for the small reserve of Dutch personnel quickly consumed by the heavy losses. In August, the squadron beat another record with 300 sorties representing 650 operational hours.

The squadron flew 265 sorties in 23 operations in September (for 675 operational hours) without any losses to report. At the end of the month, the Mitchells supported the Allied forces fighting around Arnhem. Three aircraft were slightly damaged by flak on the 25th. The first half of October was similar to September, but a major event occurred on the 18th when the squadron was re-located to the Continent and B.58/Melsbroek, north of Brussels. To prepare for the move, all operations ceased after the 7th. Melsbroek would be home for the squadron until the end of April 1945. After some time to re-organise, operations resumed on the 21st. Three days later, while attacking a road bridge at Hedel, Mitchell FR176/P was hit by flak. The crew managed to abandon the aircraft over Allied lines and returned to the squadron within a couple of hours. In November, the unit got airborne eighteen times and each time the weather was good enough to carry out the op with a good chance of success. Likewise in December, but to avoid cancelling too many operations due to bad weather, the Dutch began to use Gee-H frequently. Even then, though, on some occasions, bombing the target was still not. On 25 December,

Cdr Arent 'Kees' Witholt, the squadron's last CO, about to jump down from a jeep and take command of FR198/NO-C (displaying 101 bomb markings). This Mitchell reached this milestone in March 1945. Note also the crocodile painted next to the letter C, without doubt the nickname or callsign of FR198 based on its individual letter. FR198 would survive until the end of war with more than 125 missions to its tally, the last being flown on 2 May 1945. Witholt was a former pilot in the NEI and was flying Catalinas when war with Japan was declared. He would be awarded the DSO post-war. (André Bar)

very accurate flak was encountered while attacking a road junction. Mitchell FW193/X crash-landed on return, but the all British crew were uninjured. Another Mitchell (FR164/D) was also so badly damaged by flak that it was later declared as beyond economical repair and struck off charge. The last op of the year was performed on the 29th when a troop concentration near Vielsalm was attacked. This was also the squadron's first use of the Mitchell III. In all, for 1944, the Dutch could be proud of their efforts with close to 2,500 sorties flown. However, the losses had been rather heavy, with the consequence that reinforcements from the RAF were needed to allow the squadron to remain operational.

During the first hours of 1 January 1945, the Luftwaffe launched its Operation Bodenplatte. Airfield B.58/Melsbroek was attacked but, luckily, as far as 320 was concerned, the squadron did not suffer any losses with only two slightly damaged Mitchells that would soon be back in action. This luck was helped by the fact that, one hour before the attack, twelve Mitchells, led by the Gee-H equipped FW227/P, had been dispatched against a motor vehicle concentration near Dasburg. The operation was carried out without incident. In January, only 100 sorties were performed, mainly due to bad weather, but the rate of success rose due to the use of Gee-H. On the 13th, a sad incident occurred when FW227/P exploded over a lightly defended target. The explosion probably damaged FR181/R which was seen making a half turn before flying on its back for a few moments and going down in flames. There were no survivors. Among those killed was the first seconded Belgian, F/O G.F. Mertens, to be lost. This loss was augmented by an accident on the 22nd when FV970 was badly damaged while taxiing in from a raid. With the end of the war approaching, it was decided not to undertake any repairs to the Mitchell and it was struck off charge on 28 March. Flak remained a real danger, however, and while no Mitchell was lost to flak that month, some were hit and aircrew injured. In February, the number of sorties almost tripled, but two more Mitchells were lost on 9 February when they collided in cloud en route to the target. Of the eight crewmen involved, only two managed to escape their

Starting in December 1944, the Mitchell Mk.III was progressively introduced into the squadron's inventory. Here is HD358/NO-J with HD346/NO-V on its left. Note the latter seems to have received new paint, but the engine cowling is still in US Olive Drab. (see a previous photo).

aircraft in time. Another crewman (W/O D.P.G. Miller, a Welshman serving with the Dutch) was also killed by flak the following week. He was part of a RAF/RCAF crew flying in FR145/P. By March the superiority of the Allied air forces was complete over Germany and, with the end of the war in sight, the Allies increased their pressure and the crews were called upon more and more. That month close to 450 sorties and over 1000 operational hours were flown. Surprisingly, but fortunately, no loss of aircraft was reported. Flak was, however, responsible for the death of Sgt H. Swinnerton on 28 March. He was flying as a gunner in HD392/A, a Mitchell captained by Dutchman, Lt A.C. Hears (the two other crewmen of HD392 were Belgian and British). In April, the number of sorties dropped to 185, and, if the accident involving FR152 on the 28th is excluded (it ran into a bomb crater at Achmer and was eventually struck off charge on 3 September), the month was uneventful. FR152 had landed at Achmer in Germany (B110) in anticipation of the last squadron move which took place on the 30th. The squadron flew its first operational sortie from there on 2 May to attack a railway node at Itzehoe. The op took two and a half hours and the twelve aircraft were back home at 13.08. The squadron continued to carry out non-operational flights and would remain under the RAF until 2 August when it was passed to Dutch control.

Summary of the aircraft lost on Operations - 320 Squadron

Date	Crew	S/N	Origin	Serial	Code	Fate
30.07.43	LtCdr Willem J. RITTE		RNNAS	FR144	NO-B	†
	Kapt Albert ROESSINGH		WML			†
	2nd Lt Evert VAN'T EIND		WML			†
	LSm Willem L. BLOK	20510	RNNAS			†
	Sm Cornelis P.J.M. VAN DER DOES	90465/z	RNNAS			†
20.08.43	2nd Lt Harke NUIHUIS		WML	FR147	NO-C	-
	SLt Jan P. OELE		RNNAS			-
	PO Frits A.J. PRINSEN	20482	RNNAS			-
	Sm Dirk H.J. BORN	12899	RNNAS			-
25.10.43	Cdr Eduard BAKKER		RNNAS	FR178	NO-W	†
	2nd Lt Richard H. VAN PELT		WML			†
	PO Marius BOLK	12156	RNNAS			†
	PO Herman G. VAN HAETFEN	20481	RNNAS			†
	SLt Jan G. ROOSENBURG		RNNAS	FR162	NO-P	-
	SLt Joseph M. P. BONGAERTS		RNNAS			-
	PO Adriaan HAMELINK	20492	RNNAS			-
	Sm Wilhelmus KAUWENBERG	18179	RNNAS			-
	Sgt Cornelis J.J. BANK	21069	WML	FR166	NO-R	†
	Sgt Jan VAN DIJKEN	21067	WML			PoW
	PO Hermanes A. KAUFMAN	12023/D	RNNAS			PoW
	PO Cornelis SHOT	16327	RNNAS			PoW
28.10.43	2nd Lt Authonius J. VAN DIEREN-BIJVOET		WML	FR174	NO-K	†
	2nd Lt Cornelis VAN DER KNAAP		WML			†
	LSm Pierre F. VAN WOESIK	20506	RNNAS			†
	LSm Albert G. APELDOORN	16238	RNNAS			†
26.11.43	Sgt Johannes A. KOK	21076	WML	FR146	NO-O	†
	CPO Reginald OVERWIJN	16709	RNNAS			Evd.
	PO Johannes H.H. DE LA HAYE	14809	RNNAS			†
	LSm Dirk J. KONING	20605	RNNAS			PoW
18.03.44	2nd Lt Hendrick J. VOORSPUY		WML	FR177	NO-M	-
	Sgt Johannes VINK		WLM			-
	Sm Karel F. VAN NOUHUYS	23523/D	RNNAS			-
	LSm Markus ENGELSMA	12262/z	RNNAS			-
	Sgt Hendrik J. OT	21071	WML	FR180	NO-H	-
	Sgt Hans F. GANS	18211	WML			-
	PO Izaak POSTHUMUS	10023/D	RNNAS			-
	LSm Jacob J.G LUB	16901	RNNAS			-

Date	Name	Number	Unit	Aircraft	Code	Fate
20.03.44	2nd Lt Adriaan **Bevelander**		WML	**FR141**	NO-B	†
	Mid George G.A. **Birsak**	19310/D	RNNAS			†
	PO Johannes J. **de Jong**	20476	RNNAS			†
	LSm Wilhlemus **Kuijpers**	90532/z	RNNAS			†
04.05.44	Lt Gerard O.J.A. **Nuesink**		RNNAS	**FR184**	NO-U	-
	SLt Louis T. **Limbosh**		RNNAS			-
	PO Christiaan H. **van Offeren**	12708	RNNAS			-
	PO Pieter **de Haan**	16069	RNNAS			-
08.06.44	Lt William C. **Dobdson**		RNNAS	**FR150**	NO-K	†
	SLt Jacob **Meester**		RNNAS			†
	CPO Reolof D. **Stoffels**	16376	RNNAS			†
	PO Johannes H. **van Hagen**	13451	RNNAS			†
	SLt Jacobus A. **Ijsseltein**		RNNAS	**FR182**	NO-R	†
	SLt Gerhardus **Mulder**		RNNAS			†
	PO Petrus **Engels**	15251	RNNAS			†
	PO Theophiele P. **Mensingh**	40420/D	RNNAS			†
	2nd Lt Henri L. **Hamilton of Silveston Hill**		WML	**FR179**	NO-T	†
	Mid Wouter **Badings**		RNNAS			†
	PO Izaak **Posthumus**	10023/D	RNNAS			†
	Sm Franz M. **Kuijpers**	18182	RNNAS			†
12.06.44	2nd Lt Danië **Brand**		WML	**FR149**	NO-U	**PoW**
	SLt Willem C. **van Haeften**		RNNAS			**PoW**
	LSm Reinout P.M. **van der Heijden**	40216/D	RNNAS			**PoW**
	LSm Cornelis **Smit**	90549/D	RNNAS			**PoW**
	2nd Lt Gerrit **van der Wolf**		WML	**FR191**	NO-A	-
	PO Jan W. **Arriens**	21161	RNNAS			-
	2nd Lt Dirk **van Dijk**		WML			-
	PO Albertus J. **de Haan**	20495	RNNAS			-
13.06.44	LtCdr Johannes C. **Sillevis**		RNNAS	**FR205**	NO-O	†
	2nd Lt Harrold **Huijskens**		WML			†
	Sgt Johannes **van der Land**		WML			†
	PO George L.R. **van Leeuwen**	20485	RNNAS			†
	PO Adriaan W. **Klaasen**	15660	RNNAS			†
20.06.44	Lt Cornelis J. **den Tex Bondt**		RNNAS	**FR151**	NO-C	†
	SLt Herman C. **Luschen**		RNNAS			†
	LSm Johannes H. **Velleman**	20650	RNNAS			†
	LSm Leendert **den Hollander**	90612/z	RNNAS			†
25.06.44	1st Lt Alphons J. **Loohuizen**		WML	**FR204**	NO-F	†
	1st Lt Joost **Sluis**		WML			†
	PO Julius A.M.A. **Hielckert**	14923/D	RNNAS			†
	LSm Henry J. **Keppler**	20598	RNNAS			†
26.07.44	2nd Lt George A. **van Leeuwen**		WML	**FR185**	NO-Z	†
	Sgt Felix H. **Bloemgarten**		WML			†
	PO Bernard D. **Meijer**	30522/D	RNNAS			†
	LSm Wilhelmus H. **Willems**	90656/z	RNNAS			†
29.07.44	LtCdr Martinus J. **Stenvert**		RNNAS	**FR158**	NO-W	†
	Lt Jolle M.P. **Clay**		RNNAS			†
	PO Ferdinand E. **van Middelkoop**	12123/D	RNNAS			†
	LSm Jacobus A.F. **Brouwers**	90654/z	RNNAS			†
09.08.44	SLt Lodewijk **van den Burg**		RNNAS	**FR143**	NO-S	-
	SLt Gustaaf L.G. **Pieters**		RNNAS			-
	CPO Albertus J. **Wams**	15157	RNNAS			-
	PO Gerrit **Hofman**	13288	RNNAS			-
19.08.44	1st Lt Folkert **Bouma**		WML	**FW258**	NO-G	†
	Sgt Hugo J.H. **Seelig**		WML			†
	LSm Rudolf **Langendam**	90653/z	RNNAS			†
	LSm Wilhelmus A.H. **Melissen**	90519/z	RNNAS			†
24.10.44	F/O Dennis A. **Collett**	RAF No. 139187	RAF	**FR176**	NO-P	-

	P/O James G.L. **Kitson**	RAF No. 142462	RAF			-
	Sgt Robert B. **King**	RAF No. 1348580	RAF			-
	Sgt Arthur J. **Fowler**	RAF No. 1396758	RAF			-
25.12.44	Sgt Johannes H. **Maas**	21082	WML	**FR164**	NO-D	-
	Sgt Gerard **Claassen**		WML			-
	Sm Bob **Roll**	90632/z	RNNAS			-
	PO Hendrik **Harsevoort**	11927/z	RNNAS			-
	P/O James W. **Reed**	RAF No. 188100	RAF	**FW193**	NO-X	-
	F/Sgt R.H. **St-Arnaud**	Can./R. 171432	RCAF			-
	Sgt Raymond S. **Newton**	RAF No. 1386541	RAF			-
	Sgt Horace V. **Mehrtens**	RAF No. 1392230	RAF			-
13.01.45	1st Lt Cornelis A. **Bastiaenen**		WML	**FR181**	NO-R	†
	Mid Louis T. **Limbosh**	21153	RNNAS			†
	PO Ernst C. **van Harselaar**	15361	RNNAS			†
	LSm Johannes **van Driel**	90652/z	RNNAS			†
	2nd Lt Jan H. **Muntiga**		WML	**FW227**	NO-P	†
	F/O Gaston F. **Mertens**	RAF No. 164497	(BEL)/RAF			†
	LSm Petrous J.E. **van Dam**	90763/z	RNNAS			†
	LSm Paul H. **Peetoom**		RNNAS			†
22.01.45	F/O Georges E.M. **Clemens**	RAF No. 162407	(BEL)/RAF	**FV970**	NO-K	-
	F/Sgt Pierre E.C. **Mortehan**	RAF No. 1424925	(BEL)/RAF			-
	Sgt Pierre R. **de Wil**	RAF No. 1424960	(BEL)/RAF			-
	Sgt Joseph **Jounen**	RAF No. 1424923	(BEL)/RAF			-
09.02.45	Sgt Johannes H. **Maas**	21082	WML	**FR165**	NO-K	-
	Sgt Gerard **Claassen**		WML			-
	PO Dirk H.J. **Born**	12899	RNNAS			†
	PO Hendrik **Harsevoort**	11927/z	RNNAS			†
	Lt Adriaan **Manschot**		RNNAS	**FW212**	NO-J	†
	SLt Thijs M. **Emous**		RNNAS			†
	W/O Robert M. **Wilson**	RAF No. 1292035	RAF			†
	SLt August K. **Knapp**		RNNAS			†
	PO Armand L. **Diets**	20391	RNNAS			†

Total: 31

WML (*Wapen der Militaire Luchtvaart* -Weapon of Military Aviation)

RNNAS ranks (with the closest equivalent RN rank)
Capt: Captain
Cdr: Commander
LtCdr: Lieutenant Commander
Lt: Lieutenant
SLt: Sub-Lieutenant
Mid: Midshipman
CPO: Chief Petty Officer
PO: Petty Officer
LSm: Leading Seaman
Sm: Seaman

Dunsford 5 March 1944, some of the squadron members:

front of the bomb dolley (l-r): J.A Ijsselstein (†08.06.44), C.H. van Offeren.

Second row (l-r): T.P. Mensingh (†08.06.44), L.AW.S. Koymans, I. Postumus (†08.06.44), F.T.C. Voogt, J. Jillings, G. Mulder (†08.06.44), E.J. Wils, G.O.J.A. Nuesink aand just below him P. de Haan, A.L.A. Hissink, R. Morpurgo, H.J.E. van der Kop.

Third row (l-r): M. Quak, two unknown, F.J. Vijzelaar, unknown, J.N. Mulder.

In the cokpit: G.A. van Dam-Merrett. BAck row (l-r); W.C. Wijtman, L.T. Limbosch, H.A.I. Geraets, H.A. Rauws. (André Bar)

Summary of the aircraft lost by accident - 320 Squadron and ferry

Date	Crew	S/N	Origin	Serial	Code	Fate
	During ferry flight or external causes to 320 Sqn					
23.02.43	Donald L.A. **ANNIBAL**	-	Civ (USA)	**FR148**		†
	F/O Leslie E. **TRIPPLETT**	CAN./J.11774	RCAF			†
	Clifford D. **SAUGSTAD**	-	Civ (Can)			†
08.11.43	Guy **RECORD**	-	Civ (Can)	**FR203**		†
	F/O Frederick A. **BEYER**	AUS. 409656	RAAF			†
	Owen G. **DAVIES**	-	Civ (UK)			†
14.08.44	*Possibly ground accident at 60 MU*	-		**FR172**		-

****

Date	Crew	S/N	Origin	Serial	Code	Fate
	No. 320 Squadron					
26.04.44	1st Lt Johan N. **MULDER**		WLM	**FR142**	NO-F	-
	SLt Willem C. **WIJTMAN**		RNNAS			-
	LSm Franz **TRIELING**	10723/D	RNNAS			-
	PO Jan W.F. DE **VOS**	20496	RNNAS			-
31.08.44	1st Lt Johannes M.A. **COLLÉE**		WLM	**FR190**	NO-E	-
	Rest of the crew not reported, but safe.					
28.04.45	P/O Hubert H.E. **BEDUWEE**	RAF No. 187635	(BEL)/RAF	**FR152**	NO-W	-
	Rest of the crew not reported, but safe.					

Total: 3

B58/Moiobroek runway, near Brussels, with some Mitchells ready for take-off. Behind, more Mitchells are waiting on the taxiway. *(André Bar)*

No. 305 (Polish) Squadron (code SM)

Formed in September 1940 within Bomber Command, No. 305 (Polish) Squadron had been flying night bombing raids since then and, by the summer of 1943, it was flying the Wellington X. The previous spring, the Polish Air Force had to face up to the lack of replacement crews for its four bomber squadrons (300, 301, 304, 305). This led to the disbandment of No. 301 Squadron in April. To limit the losses, it was decided during the summer to transfer No. 305 Squadron to 2 TAF and convert from the Wellington to the Mitchell. Two Group/2 TAF had a lower loss rate per operation than Bomber Command and the Mitchell also had the advantage of being crewed by just four men instead of five meaning that losses should be easier to replace.

The administrative switch was made on 5 September and 305 transferred from Ingham, having been under 1 Group authority, to Swanton Morley. The squadron was commanded by Wing Commander K.W. Konopasek. The rest of the month was spent in training on the new mount and about sixty hours were flown. In October, practice continued, but FV911 crashed near Little Snoring while attempting a forced landing on 4 October. None of the four men on board were seriously injured, but the aircraft was a write-off. The rest of the month was uneventful and in all 145 hours were flown in October. Training continued until 4 November. The next day, four aircraft participated in *Ramrod 222* (flying with No. 226 Squadron) to Mimoyeque in France (V-1 sites). No loss was reported but the raid was not considered a success as the nearest bomb exploded 500 yards from the target. Four days later, the squadron dispatched three more Mitchells to the same target (*Ramrod 223*), but, while better results were observed, the raid was not conclusive. The squadron participated in the next two *Ramrods* (224 and 225) on 10 and 11 November respectively, attacking the same target in the

No. 305 Squadron never became fully operational and working-up proved to be difficult. The squadron never received its full complement of aircraft. Some are represented here at various stages of acceptance with codes still being painted. Above, FV913/SM-C, which was later issued to No. 98 Squadron, and, below, FV948/SM-Q with incomplete codes. The differing tones of the letters are clearly visible (see colour profile). FV948 later served with No. 226 Squadron. Both aircraft participated in the first raid carried out by the Poles, flying Mitchells, on 5 November 1943. (*Wilhelm Ratuszynski*)

Pas-de-Calais, but results could only be observed on the second raid. Besides operations, 305 continued with practice flights. On 14 November, six aircraft took off for formation flying practice, but were ordered back to base owing to bad weather. Disaster overtook when FV941 was seen in a steep banking turn before it suddenly turned over and hit the ground in a spin. There were no survivors. Four days later, the squadron moved to Lasham with its nine serviceable Mitchells, and from there two Mitchells participated in another *Ramrod* (226) on the 26th, with Sgt F. Bakalarski and Sgt T. Wolski at the controls of FV948/Q and FV976/S respectively. It would actually be the last op flown by the Mitchells as, on 3 December, the squadron received orders to cease training on the type as it was to convert to the Mosquito FB.VI. There were many reasons for the change; the shortage of flying personnel and the Poles struggling to provide the required number of trained personnel to date. It had become clear that it would be hard for 305 to become a fully operational squadron with two flights (so far only one flight had been made available for operations). Even if the Poles had been able to overcome this problem, it would have taken too long during a time when 2 TAF needed to have its squadrons fully operational. The Mosquito, of course, was crewed by just two.

Summary of the aircraft lost by accident - 305 Squadron

Date	Crew	S/N	Origin	Serial	Code	Fate
04.10.43	Sgt Zdzisław **Stępień**	PAF No. 782909	PAF	**FV911**	SM-L	-
	F/O Jan **Lemieszonek**	PAF P-1334	PAF			-
	Sgt Józef **Witek**	PAF No. 794534	PAF			-
	Sgt Wacław **Bruliński**	PAF No. 704790	PAF			-
14.11.43	F/Sgt Henryk **Anglik**	PAF No. 782801	PAF	**FV941**	SM-D	†
	F/O Walery S. **Fuchs**	PAF P-1551	PAF			†
	F/Sgt Marian J. **Andruszkow**	PAF No. 794340	PAF			†
	Sgt Jan **Twardowski**	PAF No. 703085	PAF			†

Total: 2

On 8 October 1943, General K. Sosnkowski succeeded General W. Sikorski, who died in office, and visited the unit before it became operational. Behind is Mitchell FV937/SM-K. *(Wilhelm Ratuszynski)*

More Mitchells being accepted. Top, FL182/SM-P waiting for 'SM' to be painted on. It was later issued to 98 Sqn and was never used on operations. Above, FL686/SM-O only flew one sortie (on 8 November) and, below, FV923/SM-E would be never issued again after its time with 305. It flew three operational sorties with the squadron on the 8th, 10th and 11th. (*Wilhelm Ratuszynski*)

No. 342 (Free French) Squadron (code OA)

Formed in April 1943 on Bostons, No. 342 Squadron 'Lorraine' was part of 137 Wing (comprising 88 Squadron on Bostons and 226 on Mitchells) and by 1945 was one of the two squadrons of 2 TAF still flying the type. The squadron could have soldiered on with the Boston until the end of the war, despite the clear obsolescence of the type, but when 88 was scheduled for disbandment early in April, it was clear that 342 could not be the only 2 TAF unit to fly Bostons. As there was an excess of Mitchells at the various depots, it was easy to re-equip the squadron with fourteen in a shot. All but three were Mk. IIIs and, except for a couple of them, had never issued to any unit before. The Mitchells arrived on 30 March and the next day the last operation with the Boston was flown. Intensive training commenced at once and by 3 April the squadron was cleared for operations. It was fully equipped with the required aircraft and personnel the next day. Training continued while awaiting orders for the next operations. On the afternoon of the 8th, the squadron was called upon to use their Mitchells for the first time. Twelve were tasked to take off at 15.00 to attack a concentration of troops near Sögel. Owing to short notice and the difficulties in changing the bomb load, only one aircraft took off (KJ645/B, *Lieutenant* P. Sauberli). The squadron had time to prepare the next day and in the morning twelve Mitchells took off to attack gun posts. The formation dropped its bomb load from 17,000 feet and returned without incident before the same target was attacked again in the afternoon. The squadron was on operations for the next two days but on 12 April, KJ661, flown by *Lieutnant* R. Dugot, missed its landing at Auxerre during a ferry flight and skidded into a dyke and caught fire. Nobody on board was injured. No operations were carried out until the 17th, but these halted on the 19th in preparation for the move from B.50/Vitry-en-Artois, where the unit had been stationed since October, to B.77/Gilze-Rijen. It would operate from there from 22 April until the end of the war. The French were called to participate in operations mounted on the 23rd, 24th, 25th and 26th, with all raids being flown without incident. The squadron was briefed to get airborne on the 27th, 28th and 29th, but each time the operation was postponed and eventually cancelled. On 1 May, the op was not cancelled and eleven Mitchells took off (a twelfth aborted) early in the morning to attack the airfield at Blankensee. The next day, two operations were flown, one in the morning, to a rail centre at Itzehoe, and the second in the middle of the afternoon, to the rail centre at Heide. Both were uneventful except that one aircraft had to return early due to hydraulic system trouble (FW239/H). The Mitchell jettisoned its bombs over the sea and made a successful landing despite the hydraulics being u/s. The Mitchells were unable to climb through cloud, with heavy icing conditions in layers from 1,000 feet to 18,000 feet, so the op was abandoned and the bombs were brought back. The formation landed at 19.40 to put an end to the war, which had started four years earlier in the desert with Bristol Blenheims, for 342 Squadron. The time on Mitchells had been short, just about a month, but 224 sorties were flown and 717,000lbs of bombs dropped. The squadron continued to fly the Mitchell until it was transferred to French control in December 1945.

Summary of the aircraft lost by accident - 342 Squadron

Date	Crew	S/N	Origin	Serial	Code	Fate
12.04.45	Lt Raymond **DUGOT**	Г.30233	FFAF	**KJ661**	OA-L	-
	rest of the crew or passengers not reported but safe.					

Taking command of 342 Squadron in mid-February 1945, *Commandant* G. Mentré would supervise the conversion from the Boston to the Mitchell. A pre-war regular French Air Force officer, he participated to the Battle of France flying Leo 451 bombers. After the armistice, he served the Vichy regime. Leaving 342 in July 1945, he continued to serve the French Air Force after the war.

The conversion was so quickly undertaken that some Mitchells of 342 were rushed into operations without the tactical markings being fully applied. This Mitchell III, KJ575/OA-C, has not yet had its individual letter added to the nose.

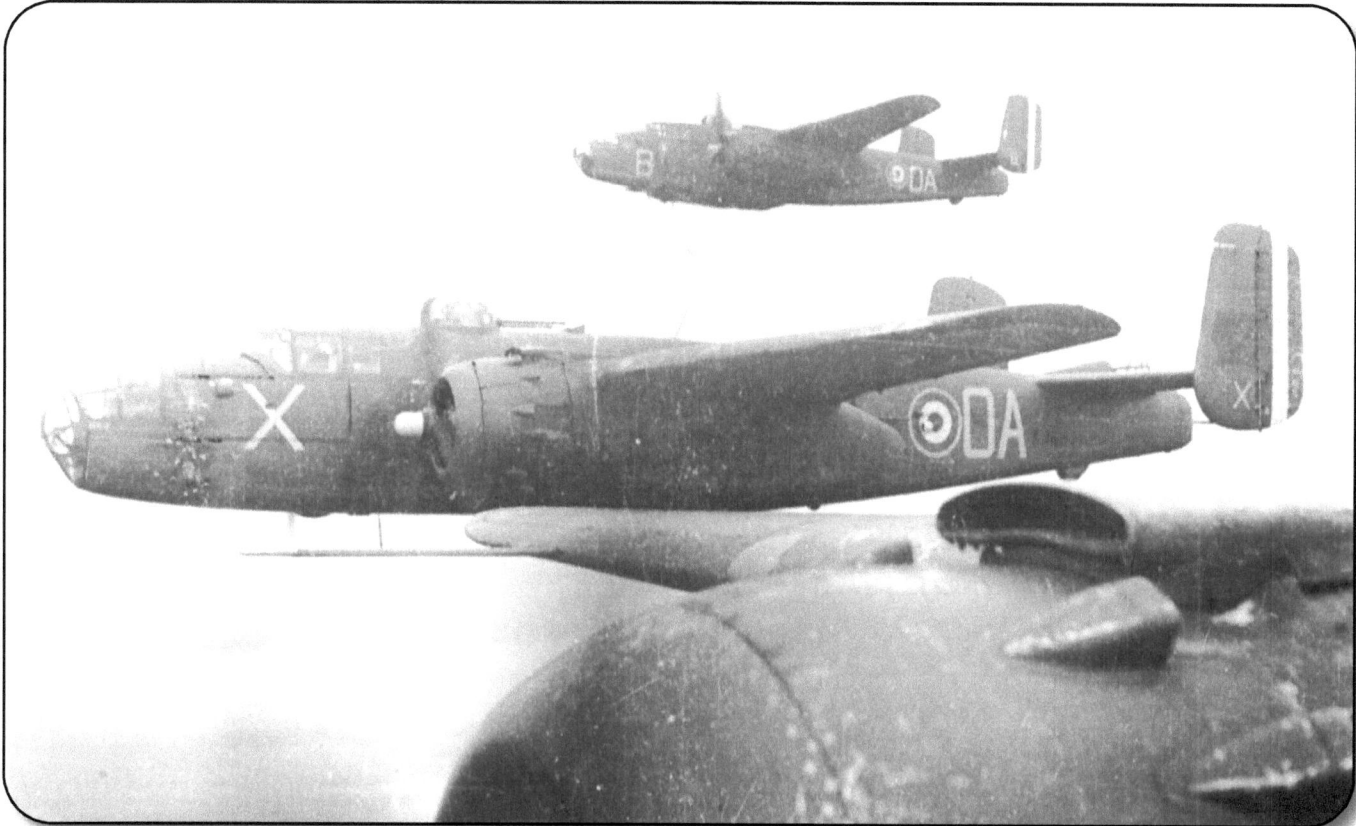

From October 1944, the French squadrons of the RAF were authorised to wear French markings so the Mitchells soon lost their RAF insignia. Above, Mitchell III KJ687/OA-X is seen in formation with KJ645/OA-B. Neither have their single nose gun installed, a weapon of little use by April 1945. Below, 342 Sqn flying in close formation to the next target. Mitchell KJ645/OA-B is again visible and, on its left, Mitchell III KJ683/OA-L.

MITCHELL MK. II - DUTCH CONTRACT
(Known number of take-offs/sorties and codes when known of aircraft made available to No. 320 Sqn)

*Total including sorties carried out with other squadrons when the aircraft was on loan.

Serials and Codes (when known)		First mission	Nbr	Total
FR141 :	320 Sqn [NO-B]	16.08.43	31	**31**
FR142:	320 Sqn [NO-F]	18.09.43	30	**30**
FR143:	320 Sqn [NO-A]	12.06.43	57	
	320 Sqn [NO-S]	15.07.44	16	**73**
FR144:	320 Sqn [NO-B]	12.06.43	7	**7**
FR145:	320 Sqn [NO-P]	04.02.45	17	**17**
FR146:	320 Sqn [NO-O]	30.07.43	22	**22**
FR147:	320 Sqn [NO-C]	12.06.43	11	**11**
FR149:	320 Sqn [NO-D]	25.06.43	49	
	320 Sqn [NO-N]	10.06.44	2	**51**
FR150:	320 Sqn [NO-W]	07.06.44	1	**1**
FR151:	320 Sqn [NO-C]	18.09.43	40	**40**
FR152:	320 Sqn [NO-W]	06.02.45	41	**41**
FR156:	320 Sqn [NO-V]	03.08.43	27	
	320 Sqn [NO-Y]	19.05.44	58	**85**
FR157:	320 Sqn [NO-X]	03.08.43	34	
	320 Sqn [NO-D]	25.02.45	39	**73**
FR158:	320 Sqn [NO-W]	03.07.44	15	**15**
FR159:	320 Sqn [NO-N]	26.07.43	58	
	320 Sqn [NO-J]	22.01.45	1	
	320 Sqn [NO-B]	22.02.45	43	**102**
FR160:	320 Sqn [NO-J]	30.04.44	54	**54**
FR161:	320 Sqn [NO-O]	21.06.44	109	**109**
FR162:	320 Sqn [NO-P]	26.07.43	16	**16**
FR163:	320 Sqn [NO-R]	21.01.45	55	**55**
FR164:	320 Sqn [NO-D]	30.05.44	73	**73**
FR165:	320 Sqn [NO-S]	16.08.43	38	
	320 Sqn [NO-K]	04.02.45	5	**43**
FR166:	320 Sqn [NO-R]	03.08.43	12	**12**
FR167:	320 Sqn [NO-V]*	06.06.44	82	**82**
FR168:	320 Sqn [NO-E]	-	-	**-**
FR169:	320 Sqn [NO-L]	17.08.43	11	**11**
FR170:	320 Sqn [NO-G]	12.06.43	29	**29**
FR171:	-			
FR172:	-			
FR173:	320 Sqn [NO-J]	25.06.43	42	**42**
FR174:	320 Sqn [NO-K]	19.08.43	15	**15**
FR175:	320 Sqn [NO-W]	25.11.43	38	**38**
FR176:	320 Sqn [NO-P]*	25.11.43	122	**122**
FR177:	320 Sqn [NO-M]	20.12.43	32	**32**
FR178:	320 Sqn [NO-W]	19.08.43	9	**9**
FR179:	320 Sqn [NO-T]	25.11.43	76	**76**
FR180:	320 Sqn [NO-H]	23.11.43	40	**40**
FR181:	320 Sqn [NO-K]	23.11.43	40	
	320 Sqn [NO-R]	16.09.44	38	**78**
FR182:	320 Sqn [NO-R]	25.11.43	74	**74**
FR183:	320 Sqn [NO-E]	23.09.44	94	**94**
FR184:	320 Sqn [NO-U]	23.11.43	48	**48**
FR185:	320 Sqn [NO-Z]	20.12.43	67	**67**
FR186:	320 Sqn [NO-B]*	26.03.44	115	**115**
FR188:	320 Sqn [NO-H]*	23.03.44	142	**142**
FR189:	320 Sqn [NO-F]*	30.05.44	91	**91**

FR190:	320 Sqn [NO-E]	20.03.44	72	**72**
FR191:	320 Sqn [NO-Y]	26.01.44	39	
	320 Sqn [NO-A]	27.05.44	13	**52**
FR192:	320 Sqn [NO-M]	10.06.44	39	**39**
FR193:	320 Sqn [NO-L]	14.08.44	104	**104**
FR194:	-			
FR195:	320 Sqn [NO-R]*	14.06.44	57	**57**
FR196:	320 Sqn [NO-T]	13.06.44	43	**43**
FR197:	-			
FR198:	320 Sqn [NO-C]	29.06.44	128	**128**
FR199:	320 Sqn [NO-N]	24.06.44	38	
	320 Sqn [NO-M]	29.12.44	61	**99**
FR200:	320 Sqn [NO-Q]	10.06.44	33	
	320 Sqn [NO-F]	09.04.45	9	**42**
FR201:	320 Sqn [NO-Z]	05.08.44	3	**3**
FR202:	320 Sqn [NO-G]	18.03.44	120	**120**
FR204:	320 Sqn [NO-S]	15.03.44	47	**47**
FR205:	320 Sqn [NO-O]	03.02.44	41	**41**
FR206:	320 Sqn [NO-J]	20.03.44	6	**6**
FR207:	320 Sqn [NO-U]	19.05.44	130	**130**

Some serials are missing from the list either because the aircraft wasn't made available to the squadron or was never issued.

Mitchell Mk. III

(the Mitchell I and II serial break-down of the remaining batches will appear in the second volume dedicated to the British squadrons)

HD346:	320 Sqn [NO-V]	29.12.44	56	**56**
HD347:	-			
HD348:	226 Sqn [MQ-]	15.12.44	7	7
HD349:	320 Sqn [NO-T]	25.02.45	9	**9**
HD350:	98 Sqn			
HD351:	98 Sqn [VO-K]	22.12.44	6	
	98 Sqn [VO-G]	20.03.45	23	**29**
HD353:	226 Sqn [MQ-G]	02.02.45	47	**47**
HD354:	226 Sqn [MQ-]	11.12.44	9	**9**
HD355:	226 Sqn [MQ-Y]	05.01.45	40	**40**
	180 Sqn			
HD356:	180 Sqn [EV-]	13.03.45	17	**17**
IID357:	226 Sqn [MQ-J]	02.02.45	47	**47**
HD358:	320 Sqn [NO-J]	25.03.45	36	**36**
HD359:	-			
HD360:	180 Sqn [EV-]	05.12.44	28	**28**
HD361:	-			
HD362:	226 Sqn [MQ-M]	02.02.45	48	**48**
HD363:	98 Sqn [VO-H]	03.12.44	10	**10**
HD364:	320 Sqn [NO-X]	13.01.45	39	
	320 Sqn [NO-H]	19.04.45	4	**43**
HD365:	98 Sqn [VO-C]	26.11.44	21	**21**
HD366:	-			
HD367:	320 Sqn [NO-G]	-	-	**-**
HD368:	98 Sqn [VO-A]	17.03.45	29	**29**
	342 Sqn			
HD369:	-			
HD370:	-			
HD371:	98 Sqn [VO-J]	26.11.44	54	**54**
HD372:	98 Sqn [VO-D]	13.02.45	50	**50**
HD373:	-			
HD374:	180 Sqn [EV-Q]	10.04.45	12	**12**
HD375:	98 Sqn			
	180 Sqn [EV-]	25.12.44	38	**38**

HD376:	98 Sqn [VO-Z]	18.11.44	55	55
HD377:	98 Sqn [VO-H]	16.02.45	26	26
HD378:	226 Sqn [MQ-D]	01.03.45	34	34
HD379:	180 Sqn [EV-]	21.02.45	28	
	342 Sqn [OA-F]	11.04.45	5	33
HD380:	98 Sqn [VO-Y]	23.12.44	10	10
HD381:	226 Sqn [MQ-L]	29.01.45	19	19
HD382:	-			
HD383:	226 Sqn [MQ-W]	05.01.45	52	52
HD384:	226 Sqn [MQ-R]	05.01.45	40	40
HD385:	-			
HD386:	180 Sqn [EV-]	06.02.45	46	46
HD387:	180 Sqn [EV-]	02.02.45	20	20
HD388:	180 Sqn [EV-]	04.02.45	25	25
HD389:	226 Sqn [MQ-E]	05.01.45	15	15
HD390:	98 Sqn [VO-U]	02.12.44	25	25
HD391:	180 Sqn [EV-]	21.01.45	10	10
HD392:	320 Sqn [NO-A]	29.12.44	26	26
HD393:	320 Sqn [NO-K]	24.02.45	11	11
	342 Sqn			
HD394:	-			
HD395:	-			
HD396:	98 Sqn [VO-K]	12.03.45	31	31
HD397:	180 Sqn [EV-]	29.01.45	33	33
HD398:	-			
HD399:	-			
HD400:	226 Sqn [MQ-A]	02.03.45	32	32
KJ561:	226 Sqn [MQ-Y]	02.03.45	31	31
KJ562:	-			
KJ563:	180 Sqn [EV-S]	04.02.45	41	41
KJ564:	98 Sqn [VO-J]	18.04.45	6	6
KJ565:	180 Sqn [EV-A]	29.01.45	18	
	342 Sqn [OA-L]	17.04.45	10	
	342 Sqn [OA-A]	01.05.45	2	30
KJ566:	-			
KJ567:	180 Sqn [EV-R]	23.02.45	53	53
KJ568:	342 Sqn [OA-R]	09.04.45	16	16
KJ569:	98 Sqn [VO-X]	25.12.44	8	8
KJ570:	98 Sqn [VO-W]	02.02.45	33	
	98 Sqn [VO-L]	24.03.45	20	53
KJ571:	226 Sqn [MQ-B]	02.02.45	42	42
KJ572:	226 Sqn [MQ-L]	03.02.45	43	43
	320 Sqn			
	226 Sqn			
KJ573:	180 Sqn [EV-]	18.03.45	12	12
KJ574:	98 Sqn [VO-Z]	24.03.45	2	2
	180 Sqn			
KJ575:	342 Sqn [OA-C]	09.04.45	9	9
KJ576:	98 Sqn [VO-P]	06.02.45	46	46
KJ577:	98 Sqn [VO-E]	23.01.45	38	38
KJ578:	98 Sqn [VO-C]	28.02.45	10	10
KJ579:	320 Sqn [NO-W]	-	-	-
KJ580:	-			
KJ581:	-			
KJ582:	-			
KJ583:	-			
KJ585:	180 Sqn			
	342 Sqn [OA-Q]	09.04.45	12	12
KJ586:	180 Sqn			
KJ587:	320 Sqn [NO-F]	13.01.45	19	19

KJ589:	180 Sqn [EV-K]	05.03.45	50	**50**
KJ590:	-			
KJ591:	98 Sqn [VO-N]	23.01.45	40	**40**
KJ592:	180 Sqn [EV-]	22.12.45	3	**3**
KJ593:	180 Sqn [EV-Y]	10.04.45	13	-
	320 Sqn [NO-T]	-	-	**13**
KJ594:	98 Sqn [VO-F]	23.12.44	5	
	98 Sqn [VO-T]	22.01.45	53	**58**
	226 Sqn			
KJ595:	180 Sqn [EV-]	02.02.45	18	**18**
KJ596:	320 Sqn [NO-Z]	16.02.45	47	**47**
KJ597:	-			
KJ598:	180 Sqn [EV-]	18.03.45	17	**17**
	320 Sqn [OA-O]	18.04.45	8	**8**
KJ599:	226 Sqn [MQ-X]	01.03.45	39	**39**
KJ600:	-			
KJ601:	226 Sqn			
KJ602:	-			
KJ603:	320 Sqn [NO-Y]	26.04.45	2	**2**
	180 Sqn			
KJ604:	-			
KJ605:	-			
KJ606:	-			
KJ607:	-			
KJ608:	226 Sqn [MQ-P]	18.04.45	14	**14**
KJ609:	342 Sqn [OA-J]	09.04.45	17	**17**
KJ610:	180 Sqn [EV-O]	23.03.45	12	**12**
KJ611:	-			
KJ612:	180 Sqn [EV-X]	11.04.45	13	**13**
KJ613:	226 Sqn [MQ-S]	02.03.45	38	**38**
KJ614:	98 Sqn			
KJ615:	-			
KJ616:	226 Sqn [MQ-V]	23.04.45	9	**9**
KJ617:	-			
KJ618:	342 Sqn [OA-K]	09.04.45	11	**11**
KJ619:	-			
KJ620:	98 Sqn			
KJ621:	98 Sqn [VO-U]	05.03.45	33	**33**
KJ622:	98 Sqn [VO-Q]	21.03.45	24	**24**
KJ623:	-			
KJ624:	98 Sqn [VO-O]	08.02.45	36	**36**
KJ625:	-			
KJ626:	226 Sqn			
	342 Sqn			
KJ627:	98 Sqn [VO-Y]	21.02.45	27	**27**
KJ628:	98 Sqn [VO-Q]	09.03.45	11	**11**
KJ629:	320 Sqn [NO-T]	17.03.45	27	**27**
KJ630:	342 Sqn [OA-T]	09.04.45	11	**11**
KJ631:	226 Sqn			
KJ632:	98 Sqn [VO-G]	03.03.45	12	**12**
KJ633:	98 Sqn [VO-X]	11.04.45	1	**1**
KJ634:	-			
KJ635:	226 Sqn [MQ-Z]	27.02.45	34	**34**
KJ636:	180 Sqn [EV-G]	10.04.45	15	**15**
KJ637:	-			
KJ638:	98 Sqn			
KJ639:	180 Sqn [EV-E]	23.03.45	13	**13**
KJ640:	-			
KJ641:	-			
KJ642:	342 Sqn [OA-G]	10.04.45	14	**14**

KJ643:	98 Sqn			
KJ644:	98 Sqn **[VO-B]**	15.03.45	20	**20**
KJ645:	342 Sqn **[OA-B]**	08.04.45	16	16
KJ646:	-			
KJ647:	-			
KJ648:	98 Sqn **[VO-J]**	17.04.45	2	**2**
KJ649:	180 Sqn **[EV-M]**	10.04.45	16	**16**
KJ650:	-			
KJ651:	342 Sqn **[OA-P]**	09.04.45	13	**13**
KJ652:	180 Sqn			
KJ653:	180 Sqn **[EV-S]**	17.04.45	6	**6**
KJ654:	-			
KJ655:	-			
KJ656:	180 Sqn **[EV-A]**	23.03.45	12	**12**
KJ657:	180 Sqn			
KJ658:	98 Sqn **[VO-H]**	21.03.45	18	**18**
KJ659:	-			
KJ660:	-			
KJ661:	342 Sqn **[OA-L]**	09.04.45	4	**4**
KJ662:	-			
KJ663:	-			
KJ664:	-			
KJ665:	180 Sqn **[EV-C]**	11.04.45	9	**9**
KJ666:	98 Sqn **[VO-A]**	09.03.45	4	
	342 Sqn **[OA-V]**	09.04.45	13	**17**

Mitchell III KJ666/OA-V 'Fort de Vaux', in the markings of 342 Sqn, wearing red codes that indicates the photo was taken after VE-Day.

KJ667:	226 Sqn **[MQ-C]**	03.03.45	44	**44**
KJ668:	-			
KJ669:	-			
KJ670:	-			
KJ671:	-			
KJ672:	226 Sqn **[MQ-E]**	01.03.45	45	**45**
KJ673:	-			
KJ674:	98 Sqn **[VO-Z]**	21.03.45	21	**21**
KJ675:	-			
KJ676:	-			
KJ677:	-			
KJ678:	320 Sqn **[NO-K]**	13.03.45	10	**10**
	342 Sqn			
KJ679:	-			
KJ680:	-			
KJ681:	180 Sqn			
KJ682:	180 Sqn **[EV-W]**	15.03.45	20	**20**

KJ683:	342 Sqn **[OA-A]**	09.04.45	5	**5**
KJ684:	180 Sqn **[EV-J]**	10.04.45	14	**14**
KJ685:	-			
KJ686:	-			
KJ687:	342 Sqn **[OA-X]**	11.04.45	12	**12**
KJ688:	-			
KJ689:	180 Sqn **[EV-F]**	10.04.45	8	**8**
KJ690:	-			
KJ691:	180 Sqn **[EV-]**	13.03.45	13	**13**
KJ692:	-			
KJ693:	-			
KJ694:	180 Sqn **[EV-D]**	25.04.45	10	**10**
KJ695:	-			
KJ696:	-			
KJ697:	226 Sqn			
KJ698:	-			
KJ699:	-			
KJ700:	320 Sqn **[NO-U]**	-	-	-
	180 Sqn			
KJ701:	320 Sqn **[NO-C]**	-	-	-
	98 Sqn			
KJ702:	-			
KJ703:	-			
KJ704:	-			
KJ705:	180 Sqn **[EV-T]**	10.04.45	14	**14**
KJ706:	-			
KJ707:	-			
KJ708:	-			
KJ709:	-			
KJ710:	-			
KJ711:	-			
KJ712:	-			
KJ713:	-			
KJ714:	-			
KJ715:	-			
KJ716:	-			
KJ717:	-			
KJ718:	-			
KJ719:	-			
KJ720:	-			
KJ723:	-			
KJ724:	-			
KJ725:	-			
KJ726:	-			
KJ727:	-			
KJ728:	-			
KJ729:	180 Sqn **[EV-]**	09.03.45	11	
	342 Sqn **[OA-S]**	09.04.45	14	**25**
KJ730:	-			
KJ731:	-			
KJ732:	-			
KJ733:	-			
KJ734:	-			
KJ736:	180 Sqn			
KJ737:	-			
KJ738:	-			
KJ739:	-			
KJ740:	-			
KJ741:	-			
KJ742:	-			

KJ743: -
KJ744: -
KJ745: -
KJ746: 320 Sqn [NO-K]   -   -   -
         98 Sqn
KJ747: -
KJ748: 226 Sqn   -   -   -
KJ749: -
KJ750: -
KJ752: -
KJ753: -
KJ754: -
KJ755: 180 Sqn   -   -   -
KJ756: -
KJ757: -
KJ758: -
KJ759: -
KJ760: -
KJ761: -
KJ762: -
KJ763: -
KJ764: -
KJ765: -
KJ766: 161 Sqn   -   -   -
KJ767: -
KJ768: -
KJ769: -
KJ770: -
KJ771: -
KJ772: -
KJ773: -
KJ774: -
KJ775: -
KJ776: -
KJ777: -
KJ778: -
KJ779: -
KJ780: -
KJ781: -
KJ782: -
KJ783: -
KJ784: -
KJ785: -
KJ786: -
KJ787: -
KJ788: -
KJ789: -
KJ790: -
KJ791: -
KJ792: -
KJ793: -
KJ794: -

Only aircraft that were made available to squadrons and entries linked with operational squadrons are listed.

✝

IN MEMORIAM

North American Mitchell Mk. II & III
Dutch, French and Polish squadrons

Name	Service No	Rank	Age	Origin	Date	Serial
ANDRUSZKOW, Marian Julian	PAF No. 794340	F/Sgt	25	PAF	14.11.43	FV941
ANGLIK Henryk	PAF No. 782801	F/Sgt	28	PAF	14.11.43	FV941
APELDOORN, Albert Gerardus	16238	LSM	23	RNNAS	28.10.43	FR174
BADINGS, Wouter		Mid	29	RNNAS	08.06.44	FR179
BAKKER, Eduard		Cdr	34	RNNAS	25.10.43	FR178
BANK, Cornelis Jacobus Johannes	21069	Sgt	25	WLM	25.10.43	FR166
BASTIAENEN, Cornelis Adrianus		1st Lt	25	WLM	13.01.45	FR181
BEVENDER, Adriaan		2nd Lt	26	WML	20.03.44	FR141
BEYER, Frederick Avery	AUS. 409656	F/O	20	RAAF	08.11.43	FR203
BIRSAK, George Gaston Andreas	19310/D	Mid	34	RNNAS	20.03.44	FR141
BLOEMGARTEN, Felix Hendrik		Sgt	24	WLM	26.07.44	FR185
BLOK, Willem Lodewijk	20510	LSm	30	RNNAS	30.07.43	FR144
BOLK, Marius	12156	PO	30	RNNAS	25.10.43	FR178
BORN, Dirk Herman Jacob	12899	PO	27	RNNAS	09.02.45	FR165
BOUMA, Folkert		1st Lt	23	WLM	19.08.44	FW258
BROUWERS, Jacobus Antonius Franciscus	90654/z	LSm	20	RNNAS	29.07.44	FR158
CLAY, Jolle Maurits Pieter		Lt	33	RNNAS	29.07.44	FR158
DE LA HAYE, Johannes Henricus Hubertus	14809	PO	23	RNNAS	26.11.43	FR146
DE JONG, Johannes Jacobus	20476	PO	20	RNNAS	20.03.44	FR141
DE PRETER, Eduard Emile George*	20252	LSm	22	RNNAS	15.08.44	FR186
DEN HOLLANDER, Leendert	90612/z	LSm	21	RNNAS	20.06.44	FR151
DEN TEX BONDT, Cornelis Joan		Lt	31	RNNAS	20.06.44	FR151
DIETS, Armand Lodewijk	20391	PO	21	RNNAS	09.02.45	FW212
DOBSON, William Castor		Lt	29	RNNAS	08.06.44	FR150
EMOUS, Thijs Martinus		SLt	29	RNNAS	09.02.45	FW212
ENGELS, Petrus	15251	PO	23	RNNAS	08.06.44	FR182
FUCHS, Walery Stanisław	PAF P-1551	F/O	24	PAF	14.11.43	FV941
HAMILTON OF SILVERSTER HILL, Henri Louis		2nd Lt	25	WLM	08.06.44	FR179
HARSEVOORT, Hendrik	11927/z	PO	26	RNNAS	09.02.45	FR165
HIELCKERT, Julius Alphons Michael Andries	14923/D	PO	20	RNNAS	25.06.44	FR204
HUIJSKENS, Harrold		2nd Lt	26	WLM	13.06.44	FR205
IJSSELSTEIN, Jacobus Adrianus		SLt	26	RNNAS	08.06.44	FR182
KEPPLER, Henry Johann	20598	LSm	18	RNNAS	25.06.44	FR204
KLASSEN, Adriaan Willem	15660	PO	27	RNNAS	13.06.44	FR205
KNAPP, August Karel		SLt	29	RNNAS	09.02.45	FW212
KOK, Johannes Antonie	21076	Sgt	25	WLM	26.11.43	FR146
KUIJPERS, Franz Matthias	18182	Sm	33	RNNAS	08.06.44	FR179
KUIJPERS, Wilhelmus	90532/z	LSm	26	RNNAS	20.03.44	FR141
LANGENDAM, Rudolf	90653/z	LSm	20	RNNAS	19.08.44	FW258
LIMBOSCH, Louis Theodore	21153	Mid	25	RNNAS	13.01.45	FR181
LOOHUIZEN, Alphons Julius		1st Lt	27	WLM	25.06.44	FR204
LÜSCHEN, Herman Christiaan		SLt	32	RNNAS	20.06.44	FR151
MANSCHOT, Adriaan		Lt	28	RNNAS	09.02.45	FW212

Meester, Jacob		SLt	20	RNNAS	08.06.44	FR150
Meijer, Bernard Dirk	30522/D	PO	22	RNNAS	26.07.44	FR185
Melisen, Wilhelmus Antonius Henricus	90519/z	LSm	20	RNNAS	19.08.44	FW258
Mensingh, Theophiele Pierre	40420/D	PO	24	RNNAS	08.06.44	FR182
Mertens, Gaston Frans	RAF No. 164497	F/O	25	(BEL)/RAF	13.01.45	FW227
Miller, Donald Philip Glyn	RAF No. 1256688	W/O	24	RAF	16.02.45	FR145
Mulder, Gerhardus		SLt	28	RNNAS	08.06.44	FR182
Muntinga, Jan Hiljke		2nd Lt	33	WLM	13.01.45	FW227
Peetoom, Paul Hendrik		LSm	26	RNNAS	13.01.45	FW227
Posthumus, Izaac	10023/D	PO	20	RNNAS	08.06.44	FR179
Ritte, Willem Jacobus		LtCdr	30	RNNAS	30.07.43	FR144
Roessingh, Albert		Kapt	29	WLM	30.07.43	FR144
Seelig, Hugo Jan Hadiwidjojo		Sgt	26	WLM	19.08.44	FW258
Sillevis, Johannes Christiaan		LtCdr	31	RNNAS	13.06.44	FR205
Sluis, Joost		1st Lt	27	WLM	25.06.44	FR204
Stenvert, Martinus Jan		LtCdr	27	RNNAS	29.07.44	FR158
Stoffels, Roelof David	16376	CPO	23	RNNAS	08.06.44	FR150
Swinnerton, Henry	RAF No. 1827820	Sgt	n/k	RAF	28.03.45	HD392
Triplett, Leslie Howard	CAN./J. 11774	F/O	n/k	RCAF	23.02.43	FR148
Twardowski, Jan	PAF No. 703085	Sgt	21	PAF	14.11.43	FV941
van Dam, Petrus Johannes Epiphanius	90763/z	LSm	23	RNNAS	13.01.45	FW227
van Dieren-Bijvoet, Anthonius Johannes		2nd Lt	24	WLM	28.10.43	FR174
van der Does, Cornelis Pieter Johannes Maria	90465/z	Sm	23	RNNAS	30.07.43	FR144
van Driel, Johannes	90652/z	LSm	21	RNNAS	13.01.45	FR181
van't Eind, Evert		2nd Lt	23	WLM	30.07.43	FR144
van Haeften, Herman Gehard	20481	PO	35	RNNAS	25.10.43	FR178
van Hagen, Johannes Hermanus	13451	PO	27	RNNAS	20.03.44	FR150
van Harselaar, Ernst Cornelis	15361	PO	23	RNNAS	13.01.45	FR181
van der Knapp, Cornelis		2nd Lt	27	WLM	28.10.43	FR174
van der Land, Johannes		Sgt	28	WLM	13.06.44	FR205
van Leeuwen, George Alexander		2nd Lt	27	WLM	26.07.44	FR185
van Leeuwen, George Lewis Rudolf	20485	PO	25	RNNAS	13.06.44	FR205
van Middlekoop, Ferdiannd Eugène	12123/D	PO	20	RNNAS	29.07.44	FR158
van Pelt, Richard Willem Hubertus		2nd Lt	30	WLM	25.10.43	FR178
van Woesik, Pierre Fortunis	20506	LSm	22	RNNAS	28.10.43	FR174
Velleman, Johannes Hendrik	20650	LSm	20	RNNAS	20.06.44	FR151
Willems, Wilhelmus Hubertus	90656/z	LSm	24	RNNAS	26.07.44	FR185

Total: 80

n/k: not known

WML - *Wapen der Militaire Luchtvaart* (Weapon of Military Aviation)

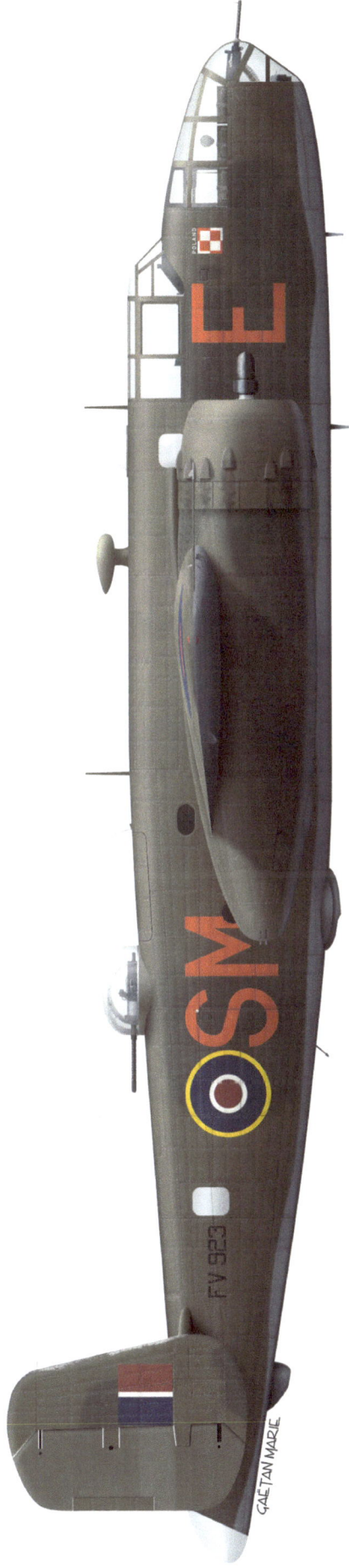

North American Mitchell Mk. II FV923
No. 305 (Polish) Squadron
Swanton Morley (UK), October 1943

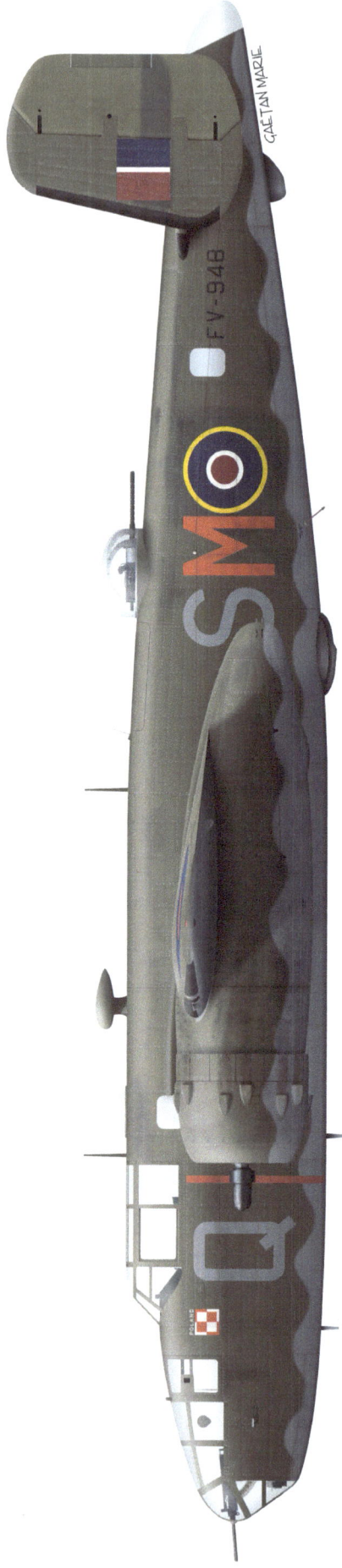

North American Mitchell Mk. II FV948
No. 305 (Polish) Squadron
Swanton Morley (UK), October 1943

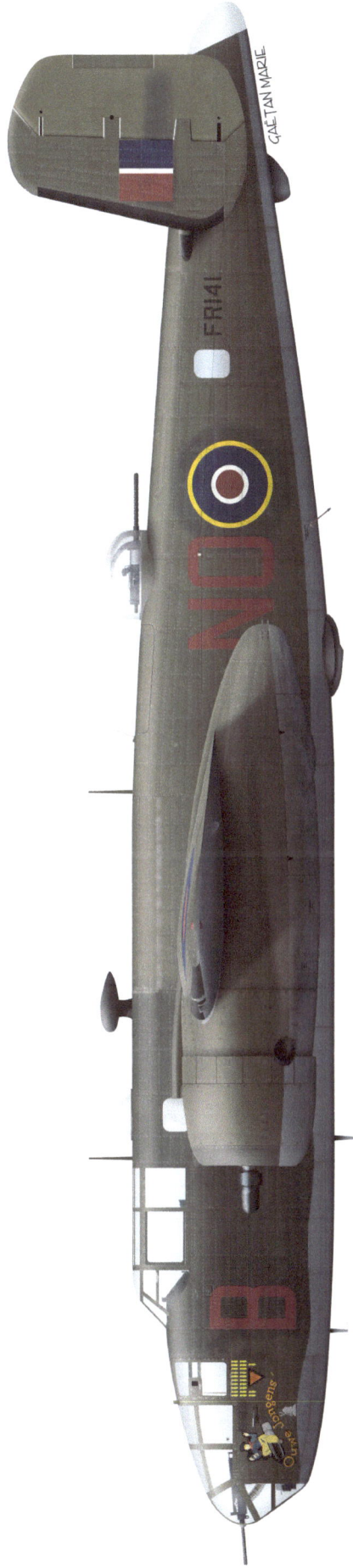

North American Mitchell Mk. II FR141

No. 320 (Netherland) Squadron
Dunsford (UK), March 1944

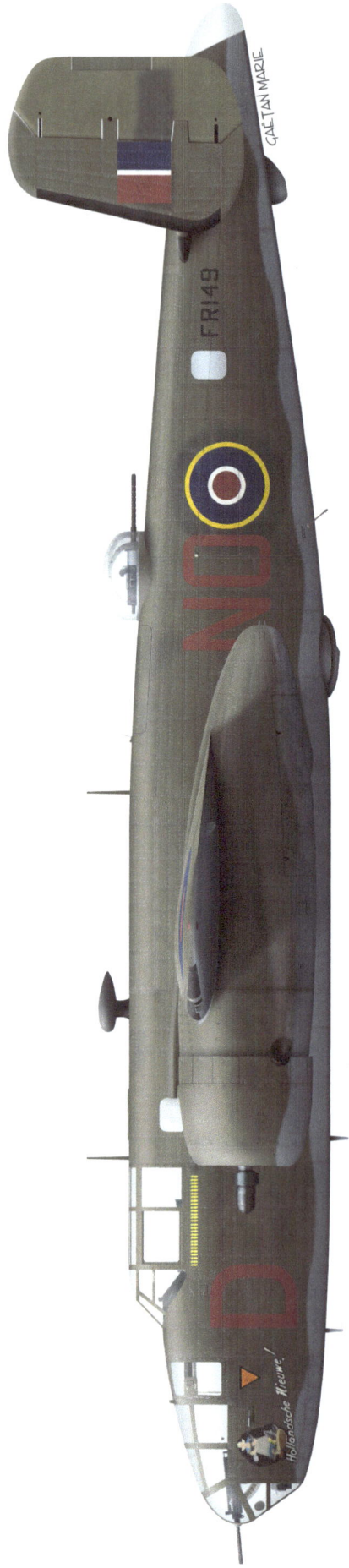

North American Mitchell Mk. II FR149
No. 320 (Netherland) Squadron
Dunsford (UK), March 1944

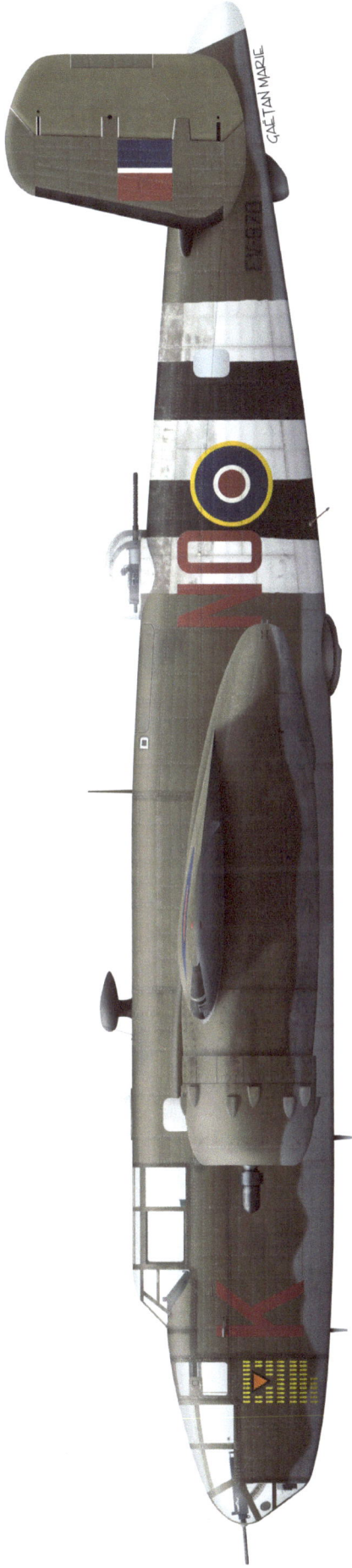

North American Mitchell Mk. II FV970
No. 320 (Netherland) Squadron
B.58/Melsbroek (Belgium), November 1944

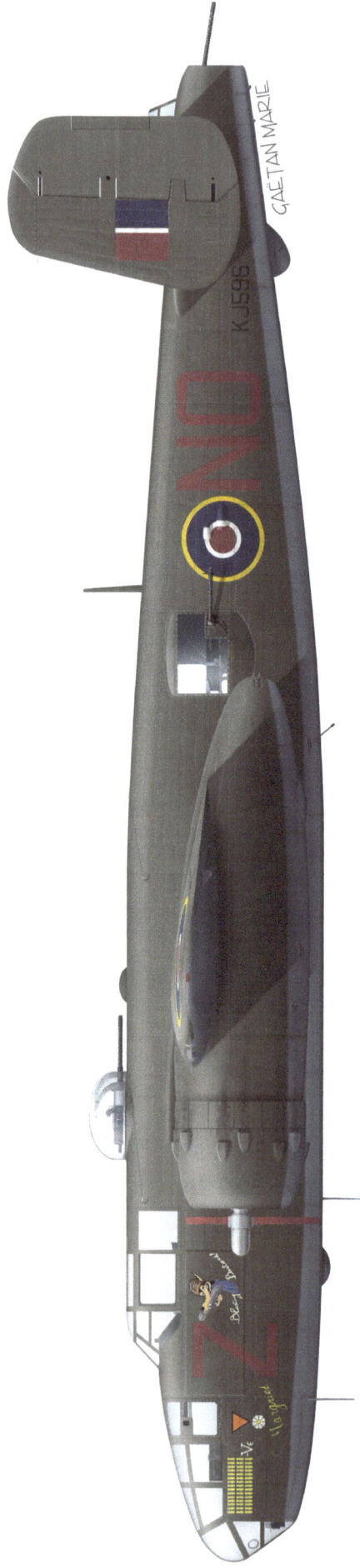

North American Mitchell Mk. III KJ596
No. 320 (Netherland) Squadron
B.110/Achmer (Germany), May 1945

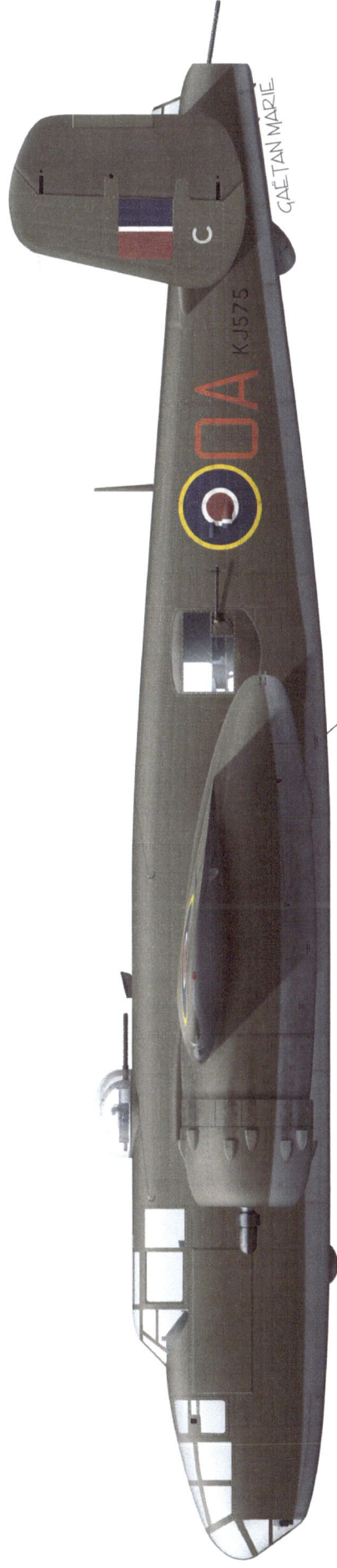

North American Mitchell Mk.III KJ575
No. 342 (French) Squadron
B.50/Vitry-en-Artois (France), April 1945

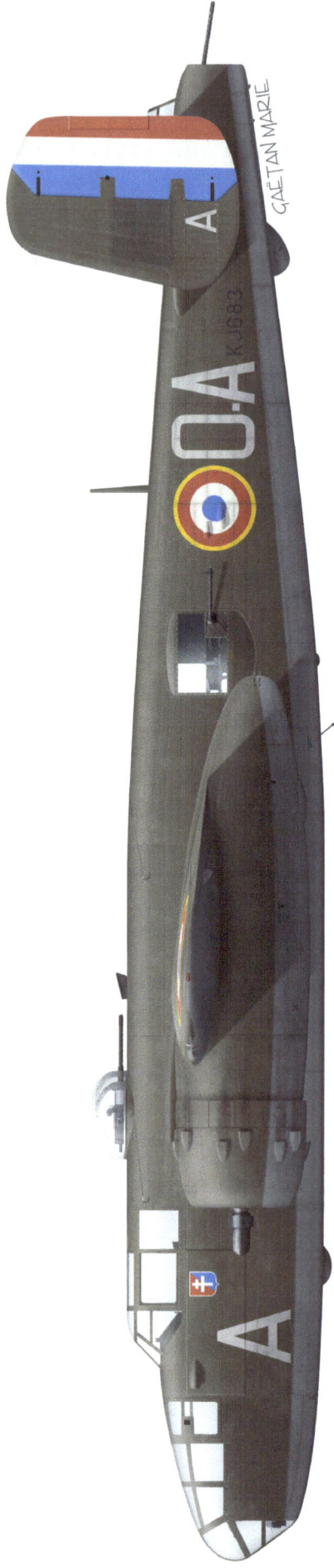

North American Mitchell Mk.III KJ683
No. 342 (French) Squadron
B.50/Vitry-en-Artois (France), April 1945

Nose arts of FR141, FR149 and KJ596

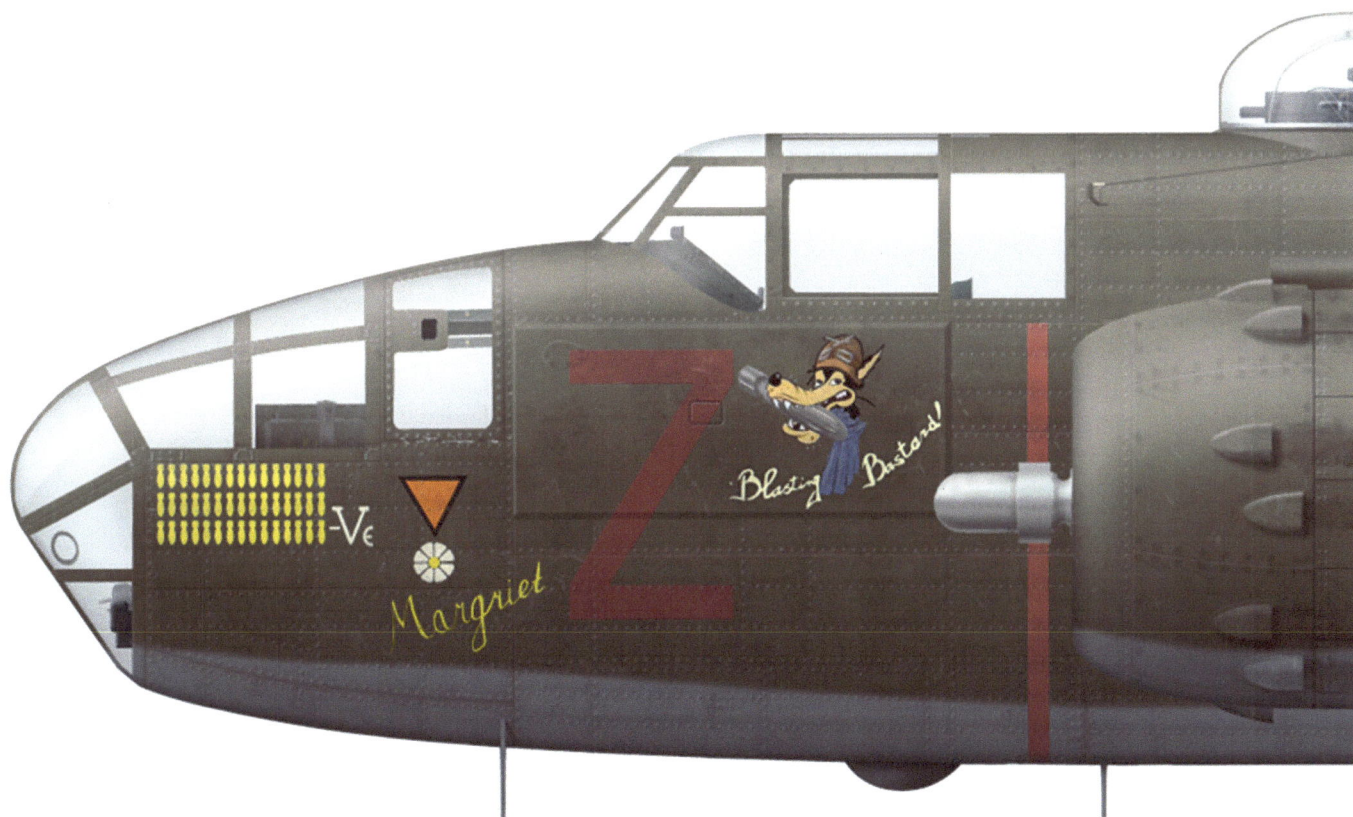

SQUADRONS! - The series

Donald James Matthew BLAKESLEE DFC
Supermarine Spitfire Mk.VB EN921
No. 133 (Eagle) Squadron
Flight Lieutenant D. J. M. Blakeslee
USA
Gravesend (UK), August 1942

Charles Cuthbertson LEARMONTH DFC
Douglas Boston Mk. III A28 w/a. A28-9
No. 22 Squadron RAAF
Squadron Leader C. C. Learmonth
No. 383
Port Moresby (New Guinea), spring 1943

Hans Anton MAURENBRECHER
Curtiss P-40N-35 CU-L-15-360
No. 120 (NEI) Squadron
Major H. Maurenbrecher
Biak (New Guinea), 1945-1946

Roland Prosper BEAMONT DSO DFC
Hawker Tempest Mk.V JN751
No. 150 Wing
Wing Commander R. P. Beamont
RAF No. 3(F)6
Bradwell Bay (UK), April 1944

Ronald Thomas SUSANS DSO DFC
North American P-51D-25-NT A68-724
No. 77 Squadron RAAF
Squadron Leader R. T. Susans
D.520
Iwakuni (Japan), 1947

James Henry LACEY DFM
Supermarine Spitfire Mk.XIV RN135
No. 17 Squadron
Squadron Leader J. H. Lacey
RAF No. 135/516
Seletar (Singapore), autumn 1945

Introducing's RAF In Combat and Bravo Bravo Aviation's collection of
highly-detailed and historically accurate, high-quality aviation prints.
For more information on available prints, please visit :

www.RAF-IN-COMBAT.com   or

BRAVO BRAVO AVIATION
BBA
HIGH QUALITY AVIATION ILLUSTRATION
WWW.BRAVOBRAVOAVIATION.COM

Prints in connection with the book:

PL-364: H Burgerhout
PL-365: K Konopasek

www.ingramcontent.com/pod-product-compliance
Lightning Source LLC
Chambersburg PA
CBHW060814090426
42737CB00002B/64